Jasmine and Stars

Islamic Civilization & Muslim Networks
CARL W. ERNST and BRUCE B. LAWRENCE, editors

FATEMEH KESHAVARZ

Jasmine and Stars

Reading More than *Lolita* in Tehran

The University *of* North Carolina Press   Chapel Hill

Designed by Kimberly Bryant
Set in Galliard by Keystone Typesetting, Inc.
Manufactured in the United States of America

This book was published with the assistance of the
Anniversary Endowment Fund of the University of
North Carolina Press.

The paper in this book meets the guidelines for permanence
and durability of the Committee on Production Guidelines for
Book Longevity of the Council on Library Resources.

Library of Congress Cataloging-in-Publication Data
Keshavarz, Fatemeh, 1952–
    Jasmine and stars : reading more than Lolita in Tehran /
Fatemeh Keshavarz.
        p. cm. — (Islamic civilization and Muslim networks)
    Includes bibliographical references and index.
    ISBN-13: 978-0-8078-3109-0 (cloth : alk. paper)
    1. Persian literature — Women authors — History and
criticism. 2. Persian literature — 20th century — History and
criticism. 3. Persian literature — 21st century — History and
criticism. 4. Nafisi, Azar. Reading Lolita in Tehran.
5. Farrukhzad, Furugh — Criticism and interpretation.
6. Parsi'pur, Shahrnush — Criticism and interpretation. I. Title.
PK6413.5.W65K47 2007
891'55099287 — dc22
2006021902

A Caravan book. For more information,
visit www.caravanbooks.org.

11 10 09 08 07   5 4 3 2 1

For SEYYED ABDURREZA FATEMI,
my uncle the painter,
who says,
"Love must *leave its*
footprint."

Contents

Acknowledgments

This delightful journey in writing would not have been possible without support from my loving family in St. Louis, Ahmet, Ali, and Ayla. Not only did they put up with my long work hours but they shared — literally — the tears and laughter that came with my jasmine and stars. My husband is the first reader par excellence of all that I write. This time my son, Ali, read too to give me a new generational perspective. I also wish to thank my sister, Fereshteh Keshavarz, whose reading of the manuscript was of great personal value.

My dear friend Safoura Nourbakhsh (University of Maryland) and her fountain of critical energy got me moving on the project and stood by me with loving support. Then entered all the wise, caring, and engaged souls we are blessed to have as our community of friends in St. Louis and elsewhere. I barely got the manuscript to the house of Sharon Stahl (Washington University) on the eve of a trip so she could take it with her. Marianne Heath (Women's League, Beirut, Lebanon) delighted me by starting to read the manuscript before even leaving my house with it. My dear Iranian American friends Mohammad Companieh and Ladan Foroughi in St. Louis both read the first draft and gave me invaluable advice on aspects of religion and culture presented in the book. My esteemed friend and colleague Jack Renard (St. Louis University) provided most beneficial stylistic and conceptual suggestions as usual. Alice Bloch (Lindenwood College) brought sensitive issues related to tone and structure to my attention. My good friends Minoo Riahy-Sharifan (Orange County) and Nargis Virani (New School) also read the first draft of the manuscript. As I carried out my final editorial revisions, my friend Joyce Mushaben (University of Missouri, St. Louis) read the manuscript with zero tolerance for textual rough edges and loose ends. I cannot thank her enough for her amazing thoroughness.

I would also like to thank all four readers who reviewed the manuscript for the University of North Carolina Press for their most constructive suggestions. In particular, I want to express my gratitude to Michael Sells

(University of Chicago), who permitted his identity to be revealed to me. Michael's insights were tremendous. They brought clarity to issues that I was aware of in a general and hazy sense. The work is much improved due to his comments.

Like most academics, I have published books before. Yet this one was no ordinary publishing experience. It was teamwork. An initial phone conversation with Carl Ernst (University of North Carolina at Chapel Hill) was seminal in the shaping of the work. Subsequent support — and ideas — from him and Bruce Lawrence (Duke University) were essential for the evolution of the book. I am equally grateful to Elaine Maisner of the University of North Carolina Press for her tremendously positive energy and unmatched professional skills. Last but not least, Jo Ann Achelpohl's assistance was crucial in preparing the manuscript for submission to the press.

This has indeed been a delightful journey in writing.

Jasmine and Stars

Introduction
What Does the Elephant Look Like?

An elephant was brought into a small town. The townspeople, who had never seen an elephant before, gathered outside the place where the animal was housed, curious as to what the beast was like. The night had fallen, and it was pitch dark, but they insisted on entering to find out as much as they could. The next day, when those who had been unable to go in asked the lucky observers, "So, what is an elephant like?" the answers were intriguing. Those who had touched the elephant's foot said, "O, the animal is like a big, thick column!" while those who had felt the trunk insisted that it was more like a drain pipe. The few who had reached up and touched the ear objected to both descriptions. "In fact," they said, "an elephant is very much the shape of a large fan."

Rumi, the thirteenth-century Persian poet, related this tale in the *Masnavi*, his major book on mystical thought. He concluded it simply to drive his point home: "If they each had a candle, they would all be looking at the same beast." The story itself is much older than Rumi. It has traveled through many cultures, each of which has created its own variation on the theme of the dangers of partial or distorted vision. It is time for us to retell the story in the twenty-first century in the United States of America to articulate one of the biggest challenges of our time. The challenge is to see each other's humanity, and the question is: where are the candles?

A cursory look around suggests ample opportunities to learn about each other. Our globe gets smaller by the day. We can now physically visit the most reticent of cultures. And new electronic means of contact develop daily: satellite images, Web logs, virtual chat rooms, text messaging, and more. E-mail is already looking outmoded and old-fashioned. And we have — proudly — chosen to name this the information age. Yet we know, deep down, that there are important gaps in what our information sources tell us about the world. This is particularly true of places such as the Muslim Middle East from which we perceive a sense of threat, though how much of a threat, and how to deal with it, we know not.

In short, since 9/11, knowing about the Muslim Middle East is not a luxury, it is a matter of life and death. We need to know if "they" and their many constellations of cultures out there are really the media-packaged, neat rows of prayer driven by faith, emotion, and instinct. We hear that some blow themselves up just so someone else might die in the process. It feels so unnatural, so wrong. Didn't these same people write delightful poetry at one time? Didn't they carve exquisite calligraphy on their window panes and even doorknobs? Didn't they welcome an exiled Jewish community fleeing Spain in the late fifteenth century? What happened? Something says we must find a candle, for there has to be more to the elephant.

We reach out to anyone who might be able to tell us something: natives exiled in the United States, academics specializing on the subject, journalists who travel the world, people conducting business in the Middle East, tourists, anyone. These are our eyewitnesses, if they care to talk about what they have seen. And some do care to talk. Whether they lived over there for years or visited for a month, whether they speak the language well or know only a few standard phrases, they do their best to describe what they saw in the light of the candle they carried or what they managed to feel in the dark.

Some of these writings are of excellent quality, academic in nature, and meant to address a very small specialized audience. Others, growing in number, are writings addressed to the educated but nonexpert reader. And the nonexpert reader is consuming these works in vast quantities, if the sales statistics are any indication. It is these nonspecialized, eyewitness accounts that I believe we need to examine carefully. They sparked the urgent need I felt to write *Jasmine and Stars: Reading More than "Lolita" in Tehran*.

In this volume, I have two specific goals. The first is to bring you an in-depth critical understanding of this eyewitness literature, which I dub the New Orientalist narrative. But the second and equally important goal is to provide an alternative approach for learning about an unfamiliar culture. Let me first tell you why I believe the proliferation of a New Orientalist narrative calls for serious scrutiny. Why do I consider this new narrative as silencing as its predecessor authored by the nineteenth-century European Orientalists?

The old Orientalist narrative, traceable mostly in the writings of European philologists, justified the colonial presence of Europe in the Eastern Hemisphere. It did not always do so by advocating a full military presence in the region (though sometimes that was stated too). Rather, it did so by narrating in clearly inferior terms everything from the language to the physiology of the natives. If something, the poetry written in the local language, for example, was too impressive to be considered inferior, it would be attributed to a glorious but discontinued past. Alternatively, a foreign source of influence would be discovered for that which appeared to be creative and complex.

Despite narrating the East in this vein, many Orientalists were devoted to the study of their subject sincerely. They studied with great care every minute detail in the semantics of the local language or in documents recording the region's historical events. But they believed—with the same sincerity—that the natives had little to contribute to a better understanding of these subjects. Indeed many felt that they knew the natives better than the natives knew themselves. Despite their scholarly devotion, through the finality of their silencing voice, they denied the locals their natural presence and psychologically dispossessed them of the intricacies of their culture.

The emerging Orientalist narrative has many similarities to and a few differences from this earlier incarnation. It equally simplifies its subject. For example, it explains almost all undesirable Middle Eastern incidents in terms of Muslim men's submission to God and Muslim women's submission to men. The old narrative was imbued with the authority of an all-knowing foreign expert. The emerging narrative varies somewhat in that it might have a native—or seminative—insider tone. Furthermore, as the product of a self-questioning era, it shows a relative awareness of its own possible shortcomings. Yet it replicates the earlier narrative's strong undercurrent of superiority and of impatience with the locals, who are often portrayed as uncomplicated. The new narrative does not necessarily support overt colonial ambitions. But it does not hide its clear preference for a western political and cultural takeover. Most importantly, it replicates the totalizing—and silencing—tendencies of the old Orientalists by virtue of erasing, through unnuanced narration, the complexity and richness in the local culture.

Some of the best-known recent examples of this narrative are in works such as *Nine Parts of Desire: The Hidden World of Islamic Women*, by Geraldine Brookes (Anchor Books, 1995); *The Bookseller of Kabul*, by Åsne Seierstad (Little, Brown, 2003); *Reading Lolita in Tehran: A Memoir in Books*, by Azar Nafisi (Random House, 2003); and *The Kite Runner*, by Khaled Husseini (Riverhead Books, 2003). I should hasten to add that these works vary in quality and deserve to be looked at individually. Indeed, if this emerging type of writing continues to grow in literary and social significance, a comparative study could be of interest. For our discussion, I will be focused mostly on what these works have in common.

While the popularity of the works I have mentioned has a direct correlation to their promise to make sense of the baffling Middle East, there is more to their success. They often have an informal tone and a hybrid nature that make for an accessible read. Most of them blend travel writing, personal memoir, journalistic reporting, and social commentary. They show awareness of the power of personal voice, nostalgia in exilic literature, the assurance that comes with insider knowledge, and the certainty of eyewitness accounts. Yet they do not demand that readers have an in-depth knowledge of the culture on which the book is focused. Neither do they provide such readers, at the end of the eventful journey, with more than a chance for a feel of the elephant in the dark. *Jasmine and Stars: Reading More than "Lolita" in Tehran* provides a closer look at this emerging literature as it unfolds its own alternative cultural perspective.

General observations about the New Orientalist narrative will not get us too far. Even universal values find their true meaning in tangible local settings. I will now turn to specifics to flesh out generality and abstraction. For this purpose, I have selected a specific title from the above list as my case in point. I will return to this example to substantiate my critique of the New Orientalist perspective as I move forward with my own narrative and arguments. The example that I have chosen is one that I feel the strongest about and am most qualified to critique, namely *Reading Lolita in Tehran: A Memoir in Books*, by Azar Nafisi (henceforth called RLT for brevity). The book has focused attention on gender issues in contemporary Iran and moved many readers with its personalized critique of totalitarianism. In the process of presenting you with my own *Jasmine and Stars*, however, I will provide a candid reading of the serious flaws in this work. Please bear in mind that my goal is larger than to quarrel with RLT. For what ultimately matters is not the irrefutable proof of the shortcomings of the feel-in-the-dark method that the book uses but the promise of my own narrative to take the reader more fully into the rich and complex world of the Middle East, to begin to read *more* than *Lolita* in Tehran. Only if my voice fills something of the existing void can I hope to have provided a candle to remove — or at least reduce — the depth of the dark. But first, how do I propose to contribute to the debate?

We are entering an era of transnationalism. This is not because compartmentalizing devices that operate through loyalty to class, nation, religion, and the like have lost their grip on us. In fact, from time to time, there are alarming indications of sharpening polarizations. But there is an undercurrent of good news that is growing stronger. We take pride in resisting authority, in being self-critical and demanding. We consider all knowledge to be partial and understand all human perspectives, insider or otherwise, to be vulnerable to personal preference, class loyalty, and political affiliation. The multiplying Web logs and virtual chat rooms may not be reliable information sources. But they have made us aware of a very important fact: the presence of other voices.

For every newly erected wall, many barriers fall down. For every newly established border, many existing boundaries lose their meaning. Exilic voices are no longer sole windows into the culture they come from. Neither are journalistic ventures into the territory of the Other few and far between. We are blessed with access to multiple voices. Recognizing the value of this multiplicity and putting it to good use is our hope for breaking out of totalizing narratives. It may not be easy to see our full human potential for crossing borders, for living outside boxes, for embracing the freedom of dwelling on thresholds. But our survival instincts tell us that good things happen when we object to becoming cogs in the system.

In the faint voices that reach us from across the globe, there is the recognition of our shared humanity. In laughing at the same joke, feeling the same pain, or admiring each other's work of art, there is an empowering flash of recognition. Through the brilliance of that flash, a voice says, "I know you are more than a number in the global statistics, because your grandmother looks exactly like mine. It doesn't matter if my Tuesday is Wednesday on your calendar. I have a little gray cat, and if you are brave enough to build a bridge, my cat and I might walk over." At times, it is hard to even contemplate the building of the bridge. But the excitement at the thought of a person and a gray cat from the other hemisphere walking in our direction is proof that we will never be totally self-absorbed or a nameless cog in the system. Not if we can help it.

This is what I am setting out to do. In *Jasmine and Stars*, I carefully and painstakingly weave a multi-hued tapestry of human voice and experience. I turn my narrating voice into a vehicle for the rainbow of the faces and words that filled my childhood and youth in Iran. I will not select any particular time period, target any specific political movement, privilege any class or gender, or handpick any specific social event. This is no ideological war for or against any. It is designed to be a meaningful excursion into modern-day

Iran: a culture as charming, creative, humorous, and humane as any. A culture that has much to offer the world.

You will laugh and cry with me and all the ordinary Iranians you will meet, some from my own family and many I could not myself have met. The compelling voices you will hear will not be those of politicians and ideologues, but of writers and poets as well as family members and friends. Some have kindled the imagination of millions of Iranians from centuries past to this very day. The rest are known only to me and a few others, but their presence has equally brightened my life.

As my narrative, enlivened with these voices, reaches out to your imagination to uphold the possibility of the bridge, there is a way to test our success. If we have succeeded in transcending the I-know-the-elephant attitude, the recognition of the multiplicity of voices will empower us to resist all totalizing and silencing efforts. We will object to the imposing vision of a revolution that stifles the power to dream. We will also object to the totalizing tendencies of a narrative such as *RLT*, which reduces the genesis and flow of that revolution to the actions of a few villains. But most important, we will begin to forge our own way of reading more than *Lolita* in Tehran, or in any place else. The trick is to listen for the seemingly insignificant voices that carry the wisdom, tenderness, beauty, and humor in a culture, to open the door and let them into the safety of our recognition. If there are brighter candles, I have yet to find them.

Let me now take a moment to explain why I have chosen Nafisi's *RLT* as exemplifying the New Orientalist narrative that I critique. This was one of the twenty-first century's best-selling titles. It was soon included in many book club reading lists and assigned in undergraduate classrooms across the nation. Most readers, however, do not know that the book has spurred a furious debate among American Muslims — Iranian Americans, in particular. Many, myself included, believe that its selective and exaggerated account of life in postrevolutionary Iran enforces a harmful, widespread stereotype of Iranians so distorted as to make them seem subhuman. To say that the book hinders intercultural exchange is putting it mildly. A critique of such damaging mispresentations of Iran is overdue.

My second reason for using this work is that, as a literary scholar who deals with texts on a daily basis, I am perplexed by the book's specific use of literature. *RLT* benefits from reading a range of good Western literature to understand the cultural change taking place in the early decades of the 1979

Iranian Revolution. However, it shows no awareness whatsoever of the lively and controversial literature created in Iran itself in the years prior to, during, and after the revolution. In fact, it suggests a total absence of interest in literature by the local culture.

Despite the intensely political arguments that RLT stirred, especially in the Iranian American community, I will not address the author's personal politics and motivation. I am interested in the making and impact of the perspective that RLT, and works of its kind, represent. As a teacher and scholar of literature, I feel we should take very seriously the distorting and silencing power that such texts exercise on our culture and society.

Persian/comparative literature and Islamic cultures are the subjects of my research and teaching at Washington University in St. Louis. Discussions and debates associated with these subjects go beyond my classroom, affecting my life and the life of the community in which I live. Like a cat carrying its newborns to safety, I hold my students close as we hunt for balanced and engaging literature that might save their critical faculty from the numbing assault of the media, particularly when it comes to discussions of Iran and Islam. The feel-in-the-dark method of describing life in Iran, evidenced in works such as RLT, further hampers the critical ability to question the narrow and slanted vision provided by the popular media.

My own contribution, *Jasmine and Stars*, is a literary and cultural analysis long in the making. I introduce you to many Iranian writers and thinkers little known in the United States, blending the presentation of their work with historical and social commentary. Yet I keep my personal voice in the foreground. Everything in the book is centered on my own personal stories, even when I reach out to classical Sufi masters to illustrate a point. *Jasmine and Stars* is a celebration of the common humanity shared among peoples of differing circumstances — religious, cultural, and geopolitical. I hope it will expose the irrelevance of prevalent stereotypes about Iranian Muslim culture.

The jasmine and stars in this book's title are metaphors for what filled my childhood and youth — which were by no means trouble free — with culturally specific inspirations that have brought me to where I am. I hope my account of the people, events, and books that nurtured me is enjoyable for you to read. More important, I hope it plants the seeds of interest in learning about aspects of Persian and Muslim life not yet known to most American readers.

I believe my readers deserve to partake of the peaceful and enriching gifts that Iran has to offer. I envision you seeking out the writings of Forough

Farrokhzad, the vibrant Iranian woman poet of the twentieth century, or Shahrnush Parsipur, the Iranian author of the novella *Women without Men*, after you read about their works in this book. I hope you read these works and enjoy them; if you are a teacher, I hope you decide to share them with your students. I even envision some of you — college students, for example — deciding to pursue the Persian language, thinking,"That way, I can read the *Conference of the Birds* for myself."

And now, more about myself. Before everything else, I am an Iranian American woman. I grew up in the historic city of Shiraz in southwest Iran, where I went to school and university. Later, I received a doctorate in Near Eastern studies from London University. I am a Muslim, a feminist, a literary scholar, and a poet, though not always in that order. I have lived and worked in the United States since 1987. I visit Iran every year and stay for anywhere from weeks to months at a time. When I am there, I see relatives, catch up with high school and university friends, buy books, visit universities and other institutions of learning, and connect with Iranian poets and scholars. Iran and America are both my home. Both make me delighted and furious at short and frequent intervals.

I have lived, studied, worked, and felt at home on three continents. If I had to define myself further, I would say I am an activist who believes we must speak and act for peace and for betterment in the world. Writing and teaching Persian and comparative literature are my academic profession, but they are also ways of attaining these ideals. I have not been employed officially in an Iranian university since the 1979 revolution and the ascendancy of the Islamic Republic. When I go to Iran for a visit, I wear the head scarf that is now mandated by the constitution. I do not wear the scarf while outside Iran, and in principle, I like people to be able to choose what they wear.

Nafisi, the author of RLT, taught literature in Iranian universities in the two decades following the 1979 revolution. For a period of time she stopped working as a sign of her opposition to wearing the head scarf. Then she returned to teaching, and her book on the Russian writer Nabokov was published by the Iranian Ministry of Culture and Guidance in 1994. Toward the end of her stay in Iran, she started a private class in her house for seven of her female students. In this class, they read and discussed world literature. RLT is centered on exchanges in this class. It is the author's account of her life experience in the Islamic Republic of Iran during the 1980s and 1990s.

I share many of the ideals cherished in this book. Gender equality, freedom of the press, freedom of the academic world, and the right of religious minorities to unrestricted practice of their faiths are among the most important. Reforming election laws would be another crucial step toward a more inclusive political space. The many Iranians who share these ideals and work hard to make them a social reality should be particularly commended for working their way through the complicated process of social and political change.

I will critique RLT in different ways, some general and some specific. Exploring the book as an example of the New Orientalist narration of social events in the Muslim Middle East, I expose its selective presentation of the Iranian people and of the cultural landscape. RLT's reductionist interpretation of the causes and effects of events is another major flaw. In my appraisal I will point to specific, short passages in the book, providing the citation for those interested in more detail. Some quotes are meant to underline shockingly stereotypical portrayals of Iranian women that might slip by an unfamiliar reader. Let me give you an example. Early in the book, one of the students shares the story of her imprisonment and flogging with the reading group. "In some perverse way," the author suggests, the punishment was a "source of satisfaction" to the young woman (RLT, 73). Harsh as the punishment itself is, RLT's comment on the incident wounds as well by stereotyping Muslim women as passive, even masochistic victims.

Faulty conceptualization of ideas is another characteristic feature of the New Orientalist narrative. RLT contains numerous examples. For instance, it explains to the reader that the concept of Muslim feminism, used by some in postrevolutionary Iran, was an invention by "the rulers" who wished to "claim to be progressive and Islamic" at the same time. The concepts of Islam and feminism — according to this view — are contradictory and cannot coexist (RLT, 262). Many Muslim feminists, in Iran and elsewhere, will find this conceptualization of feminism and Islam simplistic as well as offensive. This view erases their feminist identity. It refuses to acknowledge their commitment to gender equality on the basis of their Muslim faith. This is an example of the approach I describe as totalizing and silencing. It is comparable to that of extremist Muslims refusing to acknowledge the existence and contribution of the feminist perspective. Our globe is moving in dangerous directions. It is time to speak to each other, which will not be possible unless we recognize the humanity — and the contribution — of those who disagree with us.

Jasmine and Stars does not provide an analysis of the 1979 Iranian Revolution. But, like any discussion of modern-day Iran, it refers to the revolution on occasion. The book does not provide wholesale approval or disapproval of any group. Over the past twenty years I have found myself in agreement or disagreement with people of diverse political and religious persuasions in Iran. The good and the bad have not been always on one side.

In general, revolutions do not present their perspectives politely and peacefully. They throw them at you. Where peaceful means have not failed, a revolution does not take place. In Iran of the 1970s, peaceful means had failed. A look at the writings of major Iranian writers of the 1960s, not all particularly sympathetic to Islam, shows that they predicted the explosion as early as those years. In the poem *I Pity the Garden*, poet Forough Farrokhzad wrote:

All day,
Sounds of shattering and explosion are in the air
Instead of flowers
The neighbors plant guns and mortars in their gardens
They cover the ponds and turn them into ammunitions chases
   — the ponds do not even know it —
And the kids in the neighborhood carry little bombs in their briefcases.

Although Farrokhzad used these harsh images only metaphorically, the poem's level of anxiety, fueled by the explosive nature of the social problems, was real.

Contrary to what the feel-in-the-dark approach may suggest, the Iranian Revolution was not the *creation* of an "absolutist Islam," although religion played an important part in it. Finding a single cause of an evil nature is always the easiest way to wrap up the discussion and enter a military monologue. No amount of fictionalization of the revolutionaries and their opponents into the wicked witch and good fairies will change the social realities on the ground (RLT, 241). The hard part is to find the real issues and address them.

What is happening in the non-Western parts of the world, and in this case Iran, is a result of decades, at times centuries, of unresolved issues. While many local problems are at the root of these issues, the part that powerful nations of the world have played in sustaining — and at times exploiting — the mess is by no means negligible. These range from the outright colonization of territories and reckless pursuit of short-term economic goals to cultural illiteracy and disrespect. The resulting injustice, poverty, and totalitarianism are now exploding in our faces. The worst approach we can take to these problems is to consider them the work of the wicked witch, to be vanished with one move of the good fairy's magic wand. Ignoring voices of dissatisfaction and dissent as the scheming of the religious devil will not get us very far.

The explosive situations that result in revolutions do not go away with denial and exaggeration. They do not go away until they are understood and dealt with. But that is possible only if we consider these situations real and worth understanding. Much needs to be learned about the Iranian experience besides the tenets of Islam (although learning those would not hurt either). Focusing on extremists and caricaturing them as epitomes of ignorance — as with RLT's Mr. Nahvi, an activist Muslim student — is a form of denial. Caricatured individuals, or types, always come back to haunt their creator, who, in the heat of denial, either blows their importance out of proportion or underestimates their abilities. Nahvi shocks the author by reading Western thinkers, falling in love, and quoting e. e. cummings, none of which is expected of a villain like him. Meanwhile, the reader waiting outside the elephant's house for an eyewitness account goes home considering the demonized Nahvi the prototypical Iranian youth.

Perhaps what we need more than anything is a global cooling that would allow us to look and listen. Listening to grievances that erupt into revolutions might in fact prevent them from happening. Part of what makes the New Orientalist narrative troubling is that, through its polarized vision of the world, it denies the value of listening. Instead, it contributes to the rising heat in the fiery East-West rhetoric. The dehumanization of Muslims in the West and the diabolic representation of the West by Muslim extremists are both silencing narratives that have resulted from this heated polarization. These narratives close the door on exchange between millions and millions of people inhabiting each hemisphere. I hope *Jasmine and Stars* will be a step toward this global cooling. I hope it shows that cultures are much more than the face they make when they are angry. I hope it brings you a glimpse of the ordinary Iran, the one that smiles, the one that I have known intimately.

Let me give you an indication of what is to come. The book opens on a starry summer night in my hometown, Shiraz. It continues with memories of later years in England, where I found and published a most exquisitely illustrated Persian manuscript dated 1410.

I then introduce you to a daring and imaginative poet of twentieth-century Iran, Forough Farrokhzad, discussing her poetry as well as the way my friends and I in high school reacted to her life and death. She was the articulate voice of our rebellion. A complete section is woven around the life and personality of my maternal uncle. Now a retired army officer living in northern Tehran, he is a great artist and a greater role model in my life. Interwoven into my conversations with him are some memorable classic Sufi stories that formed the backdrop to most of our exchanges.

I also provide you with a richly detailed reading of *Women without Men*, one of the most provocative short novels written by Shahrnush Parsipur, a tremendously imaginative woman writer of postrevolutionary Iran. Parsipur, who now lives in the United States, wrote the novel in the immediate aftermath of the revolution while living in Iran. I call this section *The Fireworks of the Imagination* to underline the complex and colorful nature of the novel, which is a daring exploration of women's journey to self-discovery.

Since RLT serves as my example of the New Orientalist narrative critiqued throughout my book, I provide you with a detailed and concrete analysis of this work. A separate section is devoted to an appraisal of the structural, factual, and conceptual flaws that make RLT a prime example of this kind of narrative.

I close with a chapter focused on my father and me. With him I had the most explosive arguments and the finest poetry exchanges of my life. He was my first and best teacher of poetry. In this section, I tell you about Princess Shirin, his favorite heroine from the widely read Persian love story *Shirin u Khusraw*, and about the pair of kittens my father worked hard to save. From him I learned to admire Shirin's strength and beauty, among other things. Although we did not discuss directly the ideal of womanhood in premodern Iran, my father's high regard for Shirin taught me that sexual appeal and wisdom do not contradict each other. In this final segment of the book, I also invite you to have tea with some of my favorite Sufi saints and meet another uncle of mine, one who once lost his shoes. Throughout the book I will share numerous episodes from my latest visits to Iran.

The jasmine and stars that I have collected for you in this book are unique in the sense that they belong to my personal story. I have picked the stars from the midsummer nights in the Shiraz of my childhood and youth, and the jasmine blossoms from grandma's prayer rug where she kept them. But they are not exceptional stories. I hope, for just that reason, that you will find them wonderful.

I

The Jasmine, the Stars, & the Grasshoppers

In Shiraz of the 1960s, where I grew up, summer nights were a journey with a few clear stops. We slept in the courtyard under a sky full of stars, away from the orange, persimmon, and pomegranate trees, but still in the yard. Wooden beds would be brought out at the beginning of the summer. They would be covered first with light textured rugs and then the bedding laid on top. The first station in the night was the cotton mattress on the wooden bed a few steps away from the trees. I would lie there and just look at the sky with wonder, trying to do the hardest thing: fight off sleep just a bit longer. How could the whole neighborhood be sleeping? Most nights, there was the regular crowd of stars overhead. But once in a while there was such an outburst of glittering spots that I would just lie there enveloped in light. Then my gaze would wander around the sky in search of empty patches until my eyes could not stay open anymore. I was very young, and the problems I had then look insignificant now. Still, I did have things to sort out, and it was much easier to put them into perspective under the sky. Most things looked small by comparison anyway. Many years later, when I studied in England for my graduate degree, I missed a lot of things, most of all sorting problems out and putting things into perspective under the stars.

The next station was not a place but a voice. It was not there every night either. Some nights, close to midnight, a particular passerby walked through our alleyway and sang. I never got up to take a peek through the door to see what he looked like. I imagined him to have long hair and to wear a white cotton robe. Perhaps he was a wandering dervish, but certainly not a beggar. Had he meant to beg, he would not have come at midnight when no one was awake to give him anything. He must have gone to school, I thought some years later, because he sang poems that I recognized from my school books and my father's recitations. They were mostly about love, God, or both. But it was not the words alone that stayed with me; he sang them with a voice that was full of urgency and yet untroubled. That is what I loved most. He sang every word as if it carried the secret of the universe, and yet he sang to a neighborhood that was mostly asleep:

I am glad to be, for being is gladdened by you
I am in love with the world, for the world is in love with you

I must have been seven or eight then. I did not know much about philosophy or mysticism. For a while I did not even know that the words the singer sang were a celebrated verse by the master *ghazal* writer Sa'di of Shiraz, who lived in the thirteenth century. But I knew that he was singing about me, of that I was sure. In his singing, there was a sense of peace with the night that made me grateful for being who I was and where I was. It felt right. Some nights, just as I began to think he was not coming, his voice would start in the distance. The combination of the stillness of the trees, the pale moonlight, and his voice was magical. I would keep still and wait to hear the whole verse then drift into sleep. I never asked anyone the next day if they had heard my passing dervish the night before. It was too risky. What if they said, "Which dervish?" and somehow jinxed him out of existence? Or, worse still, they could say, "O, the dervish," and he would not be magical anymore. As long as no one talked about him, he remained my secret door to a world of comfortable sleepy thoughts.

The next station was just before dawn, and sometimes I missed it completely. I would wake up to the sound of my parents — and my grandmother if she was staying with us that night — performing their ritual wash before the dawn prayer. I had seen the ritual many times during the day. There was nothing mysterious about it. You washed the hands, face, arms, and feet. But before dawn, it was different. First, came the sound of water, then very gentle footfalls — so as not to wake us up — and then the soft whispers of the words of prayer spreading in the early morning air. This was such a short stop that I was never sure if I had really woken up. But it was an important one, particularly if I had argued with someone the day before, done badly on a test, or been scolded for something I should not have done. The sound of prayer said all was back to normal. I would turn softly — careful not to disperse the prayers in the air — and go right back to sleep.

The last station I should call the jasmine station. It was bright and fragrant, and I got the pleasure of it only if my grandmother was staying with us. She would not go back to bed after the dawn prayer. She would walk around the yard, quietly water the plants, and pick little, white jasmine blossoms from the tree that had climbed one wall of the yard all the way to the top. In summertime the tree, covered in white star-like flowers, many of which also covered the ground, looked like a bride standing on a white carpet. My grandmother somehow associated these flowers with prayer and collected fresh jasmine to keep inside her prayer rug until the next morning. But she always collected a few extra flowers for us children and left them on our respective pillows right under our sleepy noses. I would wake up first to their scent, then to their white smiles, and finally to the softness of their petals. They were not just jasmines. They were inseparable from grandma and her prayer rug. They were the gateway to busy summer days.

There were less desirable stations too. One was the arrival of the grasshoppers. Sometimes during the summers in Shiraz the sky would suddenly go dark, and worry would spread over the faces of the grown-ups. It was the migrating grasshoppers. The grown-ups worried because they knew that the wheat or vegetables in some nearby field were about to be destroyed in a matter of hours. A few days after that, many small farmers would be broke, and a few weeks later the price of fresh produce would double. I mourned the attack of the grasshoppers, even when I was not old enough to know the full sad story. I had my own reasons. I was afraid of their long, green bodies and springy legs. Plus, I hated the fact that no one understood my fear. Children in the neighborhood played with the grasshoppers, and my youngest uncle used all the psychological tricks he knew to convince me to touch them so I would lose my fear. But it did not work. Once the insects invaded the sky, I knew there would be lazy ones who would land in our yard to rest and tired ones who would fall despite their will to get to the fields. I would go inside, keep the windows closed, and be suspicious of every green spot that appeared to be moving. It took many days before sleeping in the yard would be safe, bright, and fragrant again.

If I told you only about the grasshoppers, you would never look for the stars or the jasmine of my summer nights. Especially if all you had ever heard about was the attack of the grasshoppers. That is why I am writing this book. I am piecing together a colorful tapestry of events, people, and books to give you a new picture of the place in which I grew up. Too many good things fall through the cracks in many books written about the country of my birth and the people who nurtured me. So I have decided to write one that focuses on the good things, one that gives voice to what has previously been silenced or overlooked. Ideally, it should be easy to point to the stars or to give you a handful of my jasmine so next time you think of Iran, you will remember things other than grasshoppers. But in fact it is not easy. The prevailing perceptions make it very hard for me to give you my gifts. It is as if a voice in the background, a master narrative, has told us how to imagine each other. That narrative has seeped into the fabric of our daily thought and the simplest of our interactions. To empower both of us to break out of that narrative is my challenge. Let me explain the voice in the background with an anecdote, the story of something that happened recently in my friendly hometown, St. Louis.

I was heading home after a long day's work when I stopped in a local grocery store to pick up bread, eggs, orange juice, and a bottle of vitamins. Waiting in line to pay, I spotted a woman standing behind me. She was more or less my age, very likely heading home from work, and had similar things in her shopping basket. Our eyes met for a second and we laughed. There was no need to say anything. We almost knew each other's thoughts: "You are tired, too . . . and glad to be heading home!" Then I got to the cash register, where a bubbly young girl with an extraordinary pair of green earrings was the cashier. She continued chattering with the customer who had finished paying and was about to leave. Then she turned to greet me:

— O My God! You are Mrs. Karamustafa (my married name), aren't you? I remember you. Am I saying it right? Mrs. Ka-ra-mustafa?
— Yes, you are saying it right. And you have a great memory!

I exclaimed with admiration, remembering her attempt to learn my name when she had looked at my credit card the last time I was in the store. People always try to say my name out loud and feel proud when they get it right. We were still laughing when I turned to pick up my bagged groceries and my eyes met those of the woman standing behind me. She was standing straight, arms pressed against the sides of her body, looking at me with a mix of discomfort and suspicion. What was conspicuously absent was the smile. I picked up the bag and walked out of the store without lingering on the incident or wondering what had happened. It was not hard to guess. My name had done it. After she had heard my Muslim name our similarities — the fact that we were two women more or less the same age going home after a long day — had become secondary. It was no longer funny that we had bought very similar things and had smiled at each other. My name said we belonged to two different—and opposing—worlds. That was enough to take anyone's smile away.

By the time I got to the car I had forgotten the incident. Such encounters are part of daily life; they happen too often to hold onto. Besides, feeling like a victim does not appeal to me. I am recounting the incident merely to explain what I mean by the power of the storyline in the background, the one that takes away our freedom to imagine each other. The popular eyewitness literature discussed in the introduction may not be wholly responsible for the polarization, but it adds to it significantly. Most of all, it translates the forbidding nature of the voice into soft and quasi-entertaining literature capable of seeping smoothly into the popular culture. Since we "know" what the elephant must look like, our numbed curiosity gives up on looking for a candle or envisioning the beast with any sense of adventure.

In the introduction, I described this popular eyewitness literature as branching out of what I call a New Orientalist narrative. Among the books exemplifying this narrative I have chosen to focus on one—perhaps the only one—about Iran that so many people have read: *Reading Lolita in Tehran: A Memoir in Books* (RLT). The slanted vision of books such as RLT is not to be taken lightly. Rather it should be critiqued properly to diminish its role in the escalating fear and suspicion in the background of our encounters. If you have read this kind of partial and exaggerated portrayal of Iran and its Muslim inhabitants, I would like you to know that under the same sky, on the same streets, and in the same houses there are jasmine flowers, skies full of stars, and passersby who sing about love. And yes, they are still there.

RLT is the memoir of a professor of literature who met with seven of her female students weekly to read classics of Western literature a decade or so after the Iranian Revolution of 1979. As the revolution went on outside, the marketing copy on the cover of the book tells us, in the professor's living room these young women read Nabokov, James, Austen, and Fitzgerald. And yet RLT is no simple and innocuous discussion of literature. Every reading in the book is tied together with some episodes from the lives of the students or their teacher. Sometimes the readings are sidestepped entirely and replaced with the author's personal observation on the revolution or an extended political commentary. The blurb promises the book to be an "exploration of the resilience" of these people "in the face of tyranny and a celebration of the liberating power of literature."

In fact, the book can be many things to many people. To some, it is a memoir, the personal encounters between a teacher and her students in a classroom that is her own living room. To others, it is an *episodic* encounter with the evils of extremist Islam. To yet others, who know something about the richness of life in Iran, the book is the story of a vibrant culture pushed like a genie into the bottle of the revolution. It is a very incomplete account of the two most troubled decades in contemporary Iranian history, the 1980s and 1990s. RLT is a landscape turned gruesome, the soil barren, the trees snatched away, the sky dark, and the rivers dry. Portraits of people or of social and cultural conditions should be like tapestries woven out of a hundred different threads, or like mosaics made of many tiles. When there are holes in the tapestry or tiles missing, the entire picture is distorted. Like many works contributing to the New Orientalist narrative, RLT contains a few patches of truth. In its entirety, however, it is a tapestry with many holes, a mosaic that has every other piece missing.

It is easy to underestimate the impact of texts on our lives. Inquiries by friends and acquaintances about RLT made me realize I should read the book sooner rather than later. Even then, I felt the need for providing a critique of it only after the author visited my university in the spring of 2004. In the simple events of that day, I saw the larger issues connected to the book's silencing narrative that privileged the attack of the grasshoppers at the cost of the jasmine and stars. Washington University's Assembly Series — a major speaker series designed to appeal to the broader St. Louis community — had selected the book. That in itself underlined the growing significance of the emerging Orientalist narrative. A faculty member is usually handpicked to introduce the speaker in this prestigious series. Being an Iranian woman on the literature faculty, I had been asked to make the introductory remarks. Graham Chapel, where the presentation was held, was filled with a large audience, many of them Iranian Americans. This was a rare occasion on which Iran was not being discussed as a nuclear threat, a suitable hideout for future al-Qaʿidah members, or a place in which sexual transgressors are likely to be stoned. A book about Iran was the focus of attention.

Yet there was a strong sense of ambivalence among many of us Iranian Americans in the audience. On the one hand, RLT critiqued totalitarianism and endorsed the transformative and liberating power of literature. It celebrated Fitzgerald, Austen, and James, whom so many Iranians had enjoyed — and still were enjoying — in Persian translation. But there were things in the book that shocked anyone who kept close ties with Iran, even the critics of the current regime. The teaching of Western literary works to Iranian students was presented as a groundbreaking act or as something on the order of taming the savages. The view presented was that "we [Iranians] lived in a culture that denied any merit to literary works" (*RLT*, 25). I had lived, studied, and worked on three continents, and if there was a culture in which people expressed their enthusiasm for literature more publicly than in Iran, I could not think of one. It would be difficult to live in Iran and not see that this enthusiasm was not limited to the educated elite either. How many a baker, shopkeeper, or taxi driver had I heard whispering Omar Khayyam under his breath. Now this book, which meant to celebrate the power of literature, denied and erased this most prevalent cultural behavior in the society I knew so well.

Narratives achieve their sense of closure through an inherent claim to completeness. Whether they specify that or not, by virtue of telling a story, they take responsibility for giving their readers the whole truth. If they adopt a strategy of selective narration they should underline the fictive nature of their presentation or risk becoming a tool for erasure, a kind of silencing medium. Many Iranian Americans who traveled to Iran regularly had no illusions about the need for change. But even to them, the outlandish culture portrayed by *RLT* was shockingly incomplete. Cinemas had been burnt, professors expelled students who disagreed with them, uncles who considered themselves "pure and chaste" Muslims molested their nieces, and every twelve-year-old girl was "considered long ripe for marriage" (*RLT*, 43).

In this gruesome human landscape, there were few Iranians who could be described as sensible and normal individuals. In contrast, there was no shortage of fanatical, senseless, hypocritical, and cowardly persons. For example, a blind censor decided the fate of Iranian cinema (which — if you follow international cinema — is in fact doing well). Even the revolutionary guard who came to arrest a member of the armed opposition hid behind a woman servant in the author's house for fear of being shot. Stern husbands and obnoxious brothers looked particularly deprived of humanity. Worse still, these problems were presented as results of the social changes following the revolution and particularly the revival of Islamic practice. With no reference to serious problems that plagued Iran under the Shah, the revolution itself appeared to have been motivated by a longing for fanaticism and a dislike for freedom and modernization.

In short, RLT's narration left many holes in the tapestry, depicting a culture peopled with petty monsters who cared only about religion, and in a superficial way. No wonder hearing Muslim names wiped smiles off people's faces. The standard conversation went something like this: "Have you read *Reading Lolita in Tehran*? My roommate is reading it. She says it is amazing." "Yes, isn't it?" I would think, "Nothing but marauding grasshoppers. It is truly amazing." Who could believe that under those circumstances jasmine and stars ever existed?

On the day RLT was to be introduced in our Assembly Series, I walked through the campus toward the chapel where I would make my introductory remarks. For some reason I remembered my bright graduate student Omid, who had given me RLT as a present with a worried look on his face. "Will you tell me what you think of the way she portrays Iran, Professor Keshavarz?" he had asked. I had promised him we would talk about the book in class. The doors of the chapel were open and people were coming in. "Omid must be sitting there," I thought. His parents lived in California. They had been forced to leave Iran when Omid was very young as conditions had worsened for Baha'i families in the early years following the revolution. Omid loved Iran and the opportunity to learn anything about it. Over six feet tall and largely built, he had the complexities of a young scholarly mind and the pure smile of a child. I do not remember any other student ever studying Persian with that kind of sincere passion. Once I brought him hard candy fragrant with dried jasmine from Shiraz, a gift from a Baha'i family he did not know. He wanted to travel there some day.

The chapel was now full. One could say people were "stuffed into the hall," if the language that RLT used to describe Iranian audiences attending a concert by teenage boys were to be adopted. The concert in Iran had been ridiculed. The author and her friends had tried to get out early that night so as not to be trampled by the "mob." But this eager American audience would not be the "mob." RLT reserved such pejorative terms as the "mob" and "mediocre" for performances in Iran and even suggested that the word *concert* be placed in quotation marks so that "such cultural affairs" would not be mistaken for "the real thing" (RLT, 299). Once again, to an uninformed reader, this statement erased the Iranian's love for music as it did the presence of all Iranian master musicians who performed worldwide. No, the audience in St. Louis would not be the mob. They would belong to the same category as the friends from the summer night party described a mere eight pages after the concert. These latter sat at tasteful small tables with fragile candles on terraces overlooking the pool, serving homemade wine. They were "cultured, witty, and sophisticated" (*RLT*, 307).

My thoughts were interrupted as I entered the small room behind the stage. My friend Barb, the organizer of the series, looked relieved. The faculty person responsible for the introductory remarks had arrived.

The author's presentation that day was as much about the dark deeds of the Iranian Revolution as it was about the healing power of literature. I used the five minutes that I had, and all the frankness I could pack into my welcoming remarks, to clarify a very small part of the confusion caused by the selective remembering of events in *RLT*. The audience seemed familiar with the book. But did they see that it was political commentary with a very personal bent? What they had read as a personal memoir moved between the liberty of writing fiction and the authority of an all-knowing political observer. In the process, the voices of those who could not be caricatured into seldom-smiling revolutionaries but did not empathize with the memoir's perspective either had been erased. Alas, the time and the place did not permit a fuller discussion of the resulting generic confusion.

I did emphasize that the memoir should not be read as social criticism because it did not have the space in which to provide the context for what culminated in the revolutionary explosion. I wanted the audience to hear that the dissatisfaction with modernization was not the cause for the sweeping uprisings of the late 1970s in Iran. Rather, the main culprits were the corruption of the prerevolutionary system and the absence of civil liberties. Every Iranian intellectual, I declared, knows that.

There was something else about *RLT* that had hurt my feminist sensibilities in particular. That was the fact that despite its seeming attention to women's rights, the book did not pay any attention to Iranian women currently involved in efforts geared toward intellectual and artistic expression or social change. Given its claim to gender-related concerns, its silence on women who had made an impact was among the most significant acts of erasure in the book. To remedy this, I read a long list of names of prominent Iranian women writers, filmmakers, painters, publishers, musicians, human rights activists, and more. "These women," I added, "were and still are the heartbeat of a culture that continues to live and express its passion through all forms of art within human reach."

There *was* something I could praise *RLT* for: its attention to the rich tapestry of world literature. It had made an attempt to understand the human experience that transcends religious, social, and cultural boundaries. I read to the audience the quote used in the book from Nabokov's *Invitation to a Beheading*. It referred to the instruction on the wall of Cincinnatus C's jail: "A prisoner's meekness is a prison's pride." Although I am not particularly fond of Nabokov, if I were to choose one of his works to talk about, it would most likely be *Invitation to a Beheading* rather than *Lolita*. So I picked another quote from the same novel, rule number six for the prisoners: "It is desirable that the inmates should not have dreams at all." And, thankfully, I could end with something good that RLT had brought to our attention: the uplifting and liberating power of literature. After all, Nabokov showed a keen understanding of the versatility of this liberating force when he spoke of curiosity as insubordination in its purest form.

In retrospect, there should have been a postlecture round table where the author would listen to comments from a smaller audience who had read the book with special attention. Omid, who worked so hard in the hope of learning about Iran, deserved the opportunity to ask some of his questions in person. And I could have taken off my hostess's hat to ask the question that had been on my mind all along: if world literary masterpieces are so entirely universal, what is so remarkable about reading *Lolita* in the city of Tehran? The title *Reading Lolita in Tehran* has an unmistakable undertone of Otherness to it: reading *Lolita* is something you should not expect to happen in a place such as Tehran.

An enlightening part of my experience that day was the variety of reactions I received to my introductory remarks. For some, I had been too critical and not appreciative enough toward the visiting author. Another group of people—mostly Americans—thanked me for providing something of a context for the book. Clearly, as they read the book, they had some gaps that needed filling. Members of the third group gave me a big, squeezing hug mixed with a sigh, a moment of eye contact, and a quiet "thank you!" These were all Iranians. My loving friend F. and her husband were in this group. I hugged them. F. whispered, "Every time the crowd laughed, I felt stabbed." These were laughs at instances of fanaticism or other flaws in the traditional Iranian society recounted in the author's presentation. I knew F. would feel that way. It hurt her so much that the world misunderstood "us" as simplistic and angry fanatics, as, well, the "mob." Now RLT had single-handedly affirmed this perception. And judging by the response from the audience, it had hit a responsive chord. I wanted to say to my friend, "Please don't be so hurt. It's not worth it."

❀   But I did not say it. First, it was not true. Second, it did not help. So many of us had been hurt, for so long, that the wounded feeling had become a familiar part of the Iranian immigrant experience. Some would avoid it by pretending to themselves that they had blended into American society perfectly. Others would develop a deep sense of guilt. All the misperceptions could not be baseless; something must be wrong with us. The first few times that someone had misperceived or underestimated me because of my nationality, I had been shocked and surprised. But my primary feeling, more than anything else, had been that of disbelief. Surely, it had been an odd mistake that would be cleared up in no time. Because I had expected such incidents to be rare, two of the earliest, which both occurred in England, have assumed emblematic status in the story of my life. One was sparked by a tiny silver spoon, of all things, and the other involved the signs of the zodiac! I remember the sense of duty I felt at the time to correct the misunderstandings. It was as if the image of an entire nation had been placed in my custody. I also remember them because of the naive sense of relief that I had immediately afterward: "Ok, that is out of the way. All cleared." I had thought, "Now I can get on with life." Well, those were my first days out of Iran.

❀   It was the fall of 1980. I had started my Ph.D. work on a collection of exquisite Persian manuscripts in London. The manuscripts had been purchased in Iran and India by a man who had employed eighty experts for the purpose. I always thought he must have been a very interesting entrepreneur. He had also owned the largest collection of bicycles in Europe. While I drowned myself in the fascinating details of the manuscripts, my archaeologist adviser kept busy with small objects found in excavations outside my hometown of Shiraz. These latest findings were all the more precious, because he predicted the rules would change for British archaeologists who seemed to have had no difficulty until then in getting the objects they excavated out of Iran. He had sent me a short article about a little silver spoon. It had been made in 500 BCE Iran and was the most delicate spoon I had ever seen. The head looked rather ordinary, but the handle bent over and turned into the head of a swan. Like most finely made silver things, it probably was one of a kind and belonged to an aristocratic, perhaps even royal, family. Having just been touched by the idealism of a revolution, I even asked myself how many people in 500 BCE Iran could have seen— much less used—a spoon like that? Still, I missed the home that I had left behind so much that I meditated on the spoon for a while and wallowed in the nostalgic beauty of things Persian.

The institute in which I worked on my manuscripts owned one of the best libraries on the history of science. It also housed a very nice restaurant in which people gathered for lunch in small groups. More interesting than the restaurant itself was the make-up of the ad hoc groups that formed around each table on any given day: historians of science, scholars of traditional medicine, graduate students like me working on manuscripts, librarians and curators of the various collections that belonged to the Institute. By some strange coincidence, a lovely, elderly Buddhist lady who shared our lunch table the day I learned of the silver spoon—or perhaps a day or two later—asked me if in Iran we ate our food with our hands. She explained that she knew some Muslims who did that to follow the tradition of the Prophet Mohammad. My first response was surprise. At the time, I did not know enough about Muslims in other cultures to have known about this. I knew that in Iran people unable to afford implements were likely to eat with their hands, but it was not to my knowledge something that Iranians in general did. I had certainly never associated the practice of eating with the hands with any kind of religious belief. So I explained all this carefully and added that in Iran spoons and forks, rather than knives and forks, were generally used at the table because the food was cut into small pieces before cooking. At this point, the curator of the collection on which I worked turned to me and said with a lopsided smile: "O, it is all right if you eat with hands. It is nothing to be embarrassed about." Someone to my right chuckled. Perhaps the laugh had not even come from someone at our table, but I felt stabbed, as F. would later during Nafisi's talk. I insisted on my explanation and elaborated further that the use of spoons was predicated upon the Persian diet, which included a lot of rice. The curator repeated his mocking assurance that whatever we did was okay and I need not feel ashamed of my culture! If he was trying to be friendly and supportive, it did not come across at all. Even the sweet little Buddhist lady was now trying to change the subject. I was speechless.

This was my first clear encounter with what Edward Said would define as an Orientalist perception of me. I was primitive and obviously used my hands to eat. Not only that, my short time in England had revealed to me the inferiority of my Iranian way of life, and I was embarrassed. And if that was not enough, I was dishonest, too. I was prepared to lie to cover up our shamefully primal practices! A twenty-six year old, seasoned by a recent popular revolution and very proud of my culture, I was not going to put up with the "superior" British attitude. When I got back to my desk that day, I dug up the photograph of the beautiful, hand-carved silver spoon and marched straight to the curator's office.

"Have you seen this?" I held the picture of the spoon in front of his face.

"O, no, this is beautiful. What an exquisite spoon. Where did you get it?" He most probably had forgotten the joke he had played on me at lunch altogether. I ignored the question and refreshed his memory:

"Do you know where this spoon was made?"

"Well, the caption says 500 BCE Iran. My goodness, isn't it gorgeous?" I ignored his comment again:

"Do you know when that is?"

"Yes, it says 500 B.C." He was beginning to look puzzled and somewhat suspicious.

"I don't mean the date. Do you know *when* that is?" Now he was really puzzled. "This is when Anglo-Saxons lived in caves." I fired triumphantly and walked out of his office.

He had remembered his remarks uttered at lunch for sure. But in the good old British tradition, he stayed calm. He did not revive the subject that day, nor did he say anything about the incident later. In fact, he and I became good friends. Later, he promoted my work and supported my right to publish the valuable manuscripts I found in the collection. When I go to London now to give a talk or visit friends, I make a point of stopping by his office to say hi. That afternoon, however, I wanted him to know how hurt and angry I had been. And even though we did not follow up on it, I knew that he understood my feelings, because his face went through any number of shades of purple in the few seconds before I left his office. And he never joked about such things again, not with me. Now that I think back, I know why his assumptions upset me so much. Not because eating with one's hands is such a disgrace. But because, despite all the stereotypes that I had encountered in Iran, and despite the way the Iranian Revolution had demonized America, I had not imagined the world in two irreconcilable halves of East and West. I certainly was not prepared to accept that any particular part of the world would have a monopoly on sophistication.

Furthermore, I was so upset because, even in the few months that I had been out of Iran, I was beginning to discover a pattern that I did not like at all. The pattern said that I belonged to a certain "kind" of people with special talents and shortcomings. And one thing was clear, the shortcomings far outweighed the talents. The other reason for my hurt feelings was that vague and general misperceptions of me were now crystallizing into direct, clear, and somewhat hostile silver spoon incidents one after the other. I had just recovered from a similar, though less intentionally snobbish, judgment of my abilities involving signs of the zodiac, one that I was determined to forget. This particular incident is important as a precursor to my silver spoon initiation. But more importantly, including it here gives me a chance to tell you about a beautiful and rare Persian manuscript that you might someday get a chance to see if you are interested in such things. You will see, once you put the two incidents together, how I was arriving at a sad and inevitable conclusion: whether I wanted it or not, I had entered a cultural war zone.

A week or so before the spoon incident, my friend R. had invited me to his parents' house in Yorkshire for tea. They lived about two hours outside London. His father was a retired judge and kept horses. His mother, an elegant middle-aged English woman, was a homemaker who grew beautiful roses. R. described them proudly as authentic English roses. The family had kindly invited me over to enjoy the horses and the flowers for the weekend. When we arrived, his mother was busy with her embroidery, which she left on the table in the kitchen to fetch us a soft drink. When she returned with the drinks, I asked, partly to make polite conversation and partly out of genuine curiosity, why she was embroidering a sign of the zodiac and what was her model for the design. One of the hassles of being a newly arrived foreigner — in any culture — is that people always think you cannot simply mean what you say. Anything you say sounds exotic and fairly difficult to handle. It must therefore mean something more important. She spent the next half-hour trying to explain to me what signs of the zodiac were amidst my frantic attempts to clarify that that was not my question. Finally, exasperated with her own failure to make me understand her point, she pleaded with her son, "Perhaps, you can tell Fatemeh what a sign of the zodiac is." He mumbled a few unclear words and quickly suggested that the three of us take a walk in the garden so that we could enjoy the beautiful autumn afternoon before dark.

R. was not trying to embarrass his mom. But the situation was rather awkward. At that time, I was working on a rare early fifteenth-century

Persian manuscript that I had discovered in the institute's collection. It contained a beautiful illustration of the signs of the zodiac. I studied these manuscripts for my Ph.D. research. I vividly remember the day that I took that simple manuscript off the shelf and opened it to the exquisite double-page painting right in the middle. The beauty of the painting and the possible age of the manuscript were so striking that I quickly closed the book and put it back where I had picked it up. It took me about three days to be ready to go back, pick it up, and take careful notes. I had not been hallucinating. It was real, a most beautiful double-page illustration of a horoscope, produced in Shiraz for a grandson of the world conqueror Tamerlane, known as Prince Iskandar. The manuscript was a wonder. It was dated 1410 in the colophon, which changed some of the assumptions we had about the history of painting in Iran and the reign of Prince Iskandar in Shiraz. Its mathematical calculations were of great value, as they probably belonged to the Persian mathematician, Ghiath al-Din Jamshid Kashi. Curiously, Kashi seemed to have written the manuscript in his own hand, a rare undertaking for a mathematician of his caliber and a fact that made the work all the more unique. And the double-page illustration of the horoscope was simply out of this world. It was not just that the library of the prince had provided an abundance of gold and lapis lazuli for clouds unfurling in the blue sky. The imagination and the artistry were breathtaking. The four seasons were depicted as angels carrying a crown and other gifts for the prince in four corners of heaven, and heavenly bodies appeared as men and women with different temperaments. The Sun held her golden face with both hands; Mars waved his sword; and Venus played her lute.

The institute had quickly moved to insure the manuscript for a large sum, and I had published an article in the latest edition of the *Illustrated London News* to publicize the discovery of the manuscript. At that particular point in time, I had probably studied every pedantic little detail about zodiac illustrations there was. My friend R. worked in the same institute and knew all this. That is why he felt embarrassed that his mother tried hard to make me understand what a sign of the zodiac was. It was easier to take a walk and look at the flowers, which is what we ended up doing that day. Still, I did not consider, not for one instant, firing an angry explanation at his mother. She was a very nice person who did not mean to be condescending or unkind. Nor was she teasing me. She simply did not know any better. In the years that followed, I would walk away from numerous zodiac encounters with just a sigh rather than a confrontation. Muslim emigrants to

27

the Western Hemisphere are familiar with these hurtful but perfectly well-intentioned exchanges. We learn quickly that fiery statements have to be used in moderation and even then only when faced with malicious silver spoon incidents.

The relation between these encounters and what I have described as the New Orientalist narrative is neither simple nor unidirectional. On one level, the incidents I described are a by-product of the overarching Orientalist narration of Iran and Islam exemplified by *RLT*. On another, the encounters themselves lay the groundwork for the unquestioning acceptance of such works. The bewilderment of the immigrant community is rooted in the same multidirectional flow of information and feeling. One is naturally proud of the success of a writer coming from one's culture of origin. Things get complicated, however, when the writing provides insider "evidence" that we are by and large the underdeveloped "Orientals" everyone had thought we were. That is why the hugs I received after the presentation were mingled with sighs and sad eye contact. Even my five-minute attempt at supplying a context had made a difference. It had, in a minor way, restored the injured humanity not only of those present but of many related to them who lived far away in Iran but still were an important part of the picture.

On the day that *RLT* was celebrated at Washington University, my "stabbed" friend and I were not in a clear majority. For many Iranian Americans in the audience, the negative aspects of the book were overshadowed by the fact that an Iranian writer was recognized. For once we were not exactly the villains (though not very different from them either). In the brief question and answer following the talk, one Iranian American described the day as being the proudest of her life. I, for my part, hoped that some of the questions I had raised would linger with the audience. The author wanted to have a copy of my remarks, if I was willing to send her one. But what I had to say did not fit into a five-minute presentation. And if I wrote a longer version I wanted it to be shared by a larger audience.

I have said enough about the reaction of the Iranian Americans in the audience to the book, but the issue is larger than the hurt feelings of a community. I would like to touch on two interrelated points in this regard before wrapping this up and attending to the jasmine and stars that I have prepared to share with you.

One important issue that works such as RLT raise for those of us in the academy is the responsibility of the intellectual from the non-Western world representing the culture of her origin. Such an intellectual is caught between two equally uninviting prospects. The first is pushing the less desirable aspects of her native culture under the carpet, as it were, so as to avoid its further villainization. The downside of this is depriving her readers (particularly people of her native culture) of the fruits of her knowledge and criticism. The second is criticizing — and ideally improving — her native culture at the possible cost of making it more vulnerable to political, cultural — even military — attacks from the dominant culture.

In some ways, the views portrayed in RLT may, in effect, prepare the American public for a tough line against Iran. The seldom-smiling monsters that emerge from the memoir do not seem to be doing anything other than hating, fighting, suppressing women, and trampling the American flag anyway. Moreover, their violence is not presented as an aberration but rather as endemic to the local culture, which makes a harsh move against the culture seem justified, perhaps even necessary. In the case of present-day Iran, the recent nuclear dispute adds immediacy to the sense of threat. Besides, the country itself is made up of Kurdish, Turkish, Baluchi, and other ethnicities — a hybridity that has led to immense cultural richness. In this scenario, however, ethnic diversity is frequently interpreted as potential sectarian rift, an added vulnerability. Even the country's sense of national unity, therefore, does not provide an argument against outside interference.

Another issue of importance to the intellectual from the non-Western world is her responsibility to the reader. It is not all about defending the misperceived East, Muslim, or Iranian. It is equally about the the reader, who has the right to remain open and curious about the rest of the world to retain the same curiosity that Nabokov called insubordination in its purest form. Or you might call this intellectual curiosity the joy of searching for a candle, of seeking your own personal glance at the elephant, of smiling at the person next to you in the cashier line.

Growing up in Shiraz, I took many aspects of my native culture for granted. Only after I left Iran did I realize that many of those ordinary habits and customs were tremendous privileges that I must share with my students. Yes, undesirable things were a part of life, too. I will always remember the woman who cleaned houses while pregnant and fasted at the same time. She believed God would punish her if she did not. Was it poverty, a lack of education, personal devotion? We did not know. Our entire family would mobilize to persuade her to break her fast. When the baby was born, the family watched her growth in case the fasting had hurt her. And there were worse things. A half-crazy colonel living on our street murdered his teenage daughter because he thought she had gotten pregnant. The whole neighborhood was in shock. But I also remember a poor charcoal seller whose store was ten minutes away from our house. All he ever asked was that we help his daughters with their schoolwork so that their talent would not go to waste. He was illiterate, unable to read what they wrote, but his happiness grew with the speed with which they could write.

Only after I lived elsewhere did I realize that my students can learn from the fact that our poets lived outside books and literature classes, that when I was feeling low I would visit the garden where my favorite fourteenth-century *ghazal* writer, Hafez, was buried instead of drinking or isolating myself. There, together with hundreds of other people, none particularly known to me or aware of my problem, I would walk in the garden, say a special prayer for Hafez, and put my thoughts into perspective. That is why the accusation that Iranian culture denied the merit of literature was so shocking. We did more than value the world of literature, we lived in it.

When I was about seven or eight years old and had done something very displeasing to my mother, she would press her lips together and look very stern. Next she would search her mind for a really bad punishment. Then she would settle for something relatively light like not allowing me to go out to play with the neighbor's kids for the next hour. The justification for her softness always came in Sa'di's words: "Trying to discipline a rascal is balancing a walnut on top of a dome!" She would not paraphrase or explain, just say the words aloud to herself. I did not know every single word in the poem but understood what she meant. This was true of all the other lines I heard people say around me on a daily basis. I understood them a little better every day as I grew older. In the meantime, these short quotes worked like little bridges connecting us with one another. My sister Fereshteh pouring herself a cup of tea, going upstairs, or walking out the door would say, "listen to the flute as it complains / telling the story of all separations." This is a line by the medieval mystic Rumi, the one who told the tale of the elephant. It is one of the best-known single verses among Persian speakers. Upon hearing the line, grandma would sigh, missing my youngest aunt, who lived in Tehran; my father would remember a good friend recently moved out of town; and I would simply feel connected to everyone else within hearing range. Without responding or even nodding, we would take the words in and know how the person who had said them felt. Loneliness and indifference among such moments of connection were hard to imagine.

When my mother employed Saʿdi's line about disciplining a rascal, this is what she meant: "I am upset at what you have done, but there are bigger things in life. Yes, you will be punished. But don't get too alarmed." In the absurdity of the attempt to balance a little round walnut on a huge dome, I saw the pointlessness of harsh punishments, and in its rolling down I heard Saʿdi's laughter. That is what I love about Saʿdi most, his laughter. He would not take anything too seriously, and through his words my mother — who could otherwise be very serious — succeeded in doing the same.

Last fall, I went to Iran to take care of my mother, who had had a stroke following the passing of my father. It was not surprising. They had lived together for fifty-five years. And although the relationship had seemed to us, the children, not perfectly harmonious at all times, a very strong bond connected them. She went in and out of what seemed like a semicoma despite all the medical care she received. I was desperate to connect with her. I had traveled thousands of miles in the hope of doing that and could not let her go without knowing I was there to be with her. One quiet and sad afternoon, I was alone with her. The nurse was on leave. The whole world seemed to have abandoned us. She had always wanted me to come home, and now that I was there, she was miles away. Even the leafy orange trees and the golden oranges left on them could not brighten the sad afternoon. I sat by her bed and stroked her hair for hours: "Maman, open your eyes. Please. See, I am here."

That day, I suddenly remembered Saʿdi! His name went through me like an electric wave. Why hadn't I thought of him before? Not only did my mother like his poetry, I knew exactly which *ghazals* she liked most. When I was young, we used to play a game reciting short verses in response to each other. There were *ghazals* that she would recite from memory every time. I bent over and whispered in her ear, "Maman, do you want me to read you some poetry?" I was ready to repeat the question at least three or four times. We had to. Even then, she did not always respond. She nodded at once. I ran to my father's old bookcase, now dusty and neglected. "Where are you, Saʿdi?" I thought. I found the collection, quickly dusted it, and planted myself on my mother's bedside, as close to her as I could get. As I started to read, her breathing got deeper and deeper and at times turned into sighs. I knew she was listening. The laughing master was not balancing a walnut on a dome in the *ghazal* I was reading. Now he was in love, which did not mean he could not tease the reader, or the beloved for that matter:

> Ecstatic with love
> Someday, I'll find my way to those lovely curls.
> Of your sweet lips alone
> I will tell a hundred savory tales
>
> Do you wish to be unkind?
> Here, I have only one life, consider it yours!
> — Or if you want me to stay —
> I'll spread it like a carpet beneath your feet.
>
> You say "Sit in sorrow till the end of your days!
> Or, rise, and give yourself to love!"
> Whatever you say my dear! I'll sit and rise
> And sit,
> And rise . . .

Then something strange and unusual happened, my mother's lips began to move. My first thoughts were, "I got carried away and tired her. I read too much. She wants me to stop." Her voice was too weak but she insisted on saying it. I bent over her bed, asked her to repeat many times, and tried to listen as closely as I could. Maybe she was hungry or thirsty at last. "No one says it as beautifully as he does. Do they?" she whispered. "No, Mom, they don't!" I murmured. She was commenting on Sa'di's poetry. I kissed her pale forehead, and tears rolled down my face. She knew I was there; we had connected. After all, what was a stroke to keep Sa'di away?

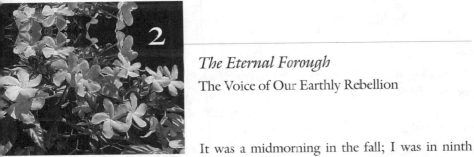

The Eternal Forough
The Voice of Our Earthly Rebellion

It was a midmorning in the fall; I was in ninth grade. As our physics teacher walked in, we knew something really disastrous had happened. Mr. N. was a demanding teacher and one who had a broad definition of teaching. While he taught his physics lessons conscientiously, he somehow found the time to talk about a lot more. "Who has read *The Grapes of Wrath*?" he would say, out of the blue, at the end of a class. Then he would use the opportunity to talk about Steinbeck. Or he might ask, "Do you read the daily paper?" This usually meant that some recent event was worth discussing. There were three or four of us who always had a short poem handy because he sometimes suggested we end a difficult lesson with a poem. Everyone liked Mr. N., even those who did not do well in physics. Once he asked if someone would like to impersonate him; to my amazement two hands shot up in the air instantly. He was delighted.

The day Mr. N walked in with a stern look on his face, our first thought was that we had done terribly on the last quiz. He stood next to the tall podium and rested his elbow on it. I remember vividly the beige suit he was wearing because it contrasted with the gloomy look on his face. It had to be worse than a bad quiz. "Something terrible has happened," he said in a low voice. "Forough Farrokhzad has died in a car accident." What? That was impossible. Farrokhzad was my favorite poet, a woman in her midthirties, and she had been so alive. Someone to the right of me gasped. The rest of us were just stunned. Mr. N. went on to say that she had hit a lamppost in an attempt to avoid running over a stray dog. Since the car was a jeep without front doors, she had been thrown out. She had died of a head injury. To this day I am not sure if this oft-repeated account of how Farrokhzad died is accurate. But her status as a beloved poet made her worthy of the velvety cloak of invented stories.

To us, in ninth grade, the story made perfect sense. Farrokhzad was in real life the same as she had been in her poetry — bold, imaginative, curious, full of the urge to live, and certainly not afraid of death. Her passionate love affair with Ibrahim Gulestan, a man to whom she was not married, had aroused anger and admiration both. But she was so much more than that love affair. In her poetic art, she had been inspired by Nima Yushij, who had lived in the early decades of the twentieth century and was known as the founding father of modern Persian poetry. She had admired Nima for breaking the rules of prosody and modernizing the old metric structure. But in a general poetic sense, she had gone much further. She—and a few other poets of her generation—had revitalized Persian poetry by opening up its thematic horizons. Thanks to them subjects as simple as smoking a cigarette and walking home with a basket of fruit, or as complicated as the horrors of intellectual inertia and the intricacies of womanhood, were now considered worthy of poetry.

Farrokhzad celebrated the fullness of her personhood, sexuality included. A radio show host once tried to get a statement out of her on the reasons why she cared so much about women's issues. She replied, "Oh, that's because I am a woman." That was the end of that discussion. In general, she had little patience for pretentious self-display or surrender to any kind of propaganda about reliving our glorious past. Her sharpest and darkest poetic humor was reserved for the inept intelligentsia of her time, given to empty talk over drink and smoke:

> So, these quiet foot soldiers leaning against their wooden spears
>   are those swift riders?
> And these emaciated opium addicts are those pure Sufis with exalted
>   thoughts?
> It is true then, that humanity does not await an arrival any more.

She fiercely fought the old, the rotten, and the corrupt yet felt unashamed of the culture in which she lived. Speaking in an unsuppressed voice, living out her creative impulse, having a room of her own, and being respected were points on which she did not compromise. Later, one of my professors who had met her told me that Farrokhzad had a shy personality. That did not surprise me a bit. She did not need to be loud. It was simply impossible to speak of her and oppression in the same breath. Her very robust presence defied oppression. Rooted in the earth, she spoke with the simplicity, freshness, and strength of nature:

I have never desired
To be a star in the mirage of the sky
Or, like the soul of the chosen ones, be a companion for angels
I have never been detached from the earth, never acquainted with the
  stars.

Standing on the soil
My body — like a green shoot —
Drinks the sun, the rain, and the wind
To live.

Part of nature's attraction was in its uninhibited desire to live, a desire that she described in another poem as "madly living" in one moment. Playing it safe was obviously not the best way to experience this eternity pressed into one instant.

In her dislike for playing it safe, Farrokhzad had developed a habit of colliding with life. This time, the collision had been fatal. She had died. That midmorning in ninth grade, we sat in stunned silence in that simple classroom. My rather shabby-looking middle school was in southern Shiraz. There were probably thirty to thirty-five of us in that classroom, all girls. Our families were not destitute, but not rich either. None of us had a lot of money to spend in bookstores, go to cultural events, or travel extensively. Likely most of our parents did not have university educations. And yet, now that I think about that day, the most amazing part of it was not that a physics teacher considered it important to share the news of a poet's death with his fifteen-year-old students. The most amazing thing is that when he announced Farrokhzad's death not a single one of us said, "Who is Forough Farrokhzad?" No doubt some of us had read her more extensively than others, but everyone knew who she was. And everyone knew how significant it was that we had lost a poet of her caliber so young.

The cry of pain caused by the loss of Farrokhzad went beyond my physics classroom. Volumes were published in her honor, and even those who had criticized her fiercely for living an unconventional life agreed to forgive her. She was accorded all kinds of epithets, the most famous among them being *Javdaneh Forugh*. *Javdaneh* means eternal and *Forugh* means light. Zoroastrian Iranians, whose religion is thousands of years old, keep their sacred fire burning. This is the "eternal fire," carrying the symbolic warmth and glow of goodness and driving away dark shadows. A halo had already begun to form around Farrokhzad's head. I am not sure who called her the Eternal Forough for the first time. But her other designation, *pari shadokht e she're aadamian*, or "the Fairy Princess of the poetry of humans," was given to her by Akhavan Saless, himself a celebrated poet. This latter indicated a legendary artistic pedigree. So much for insisting on remaining earthly! Perhaps she was a fairy princess for that very reason. Indeed, this would be an exceptional fairy princess, one whose robust presence did not remain captive to legends. Farrokhzad's earthly voice, echoed in edition after edition, was to dominate modern Persian poetry.

For a poet to attain this kind of social presence and widespread recognition is striking in any culture. When the poet is a Middle Eastern woman, normally portrayed as passive and silent, it ought to be even more worthy of comment. A book celebrating the power of literature, set in contemporary Iran, and written by a professor of literature — all of which describe *Reading Lolita in Tehran* (RLT) — would seem to be the most likely source for reading about an Iranian woman poet of Farrokhzad's import. However, the book remains silent about Farrokhzad — and women like her — instead presenting Iranian women's lot in life as one inevitably filled with suffering and victimization. The silencing nature of the New Orientalist narrative overlooks these women's contributions.

Not only can you read a book such as RLT and not have any idea that a voice as feminine, strong, and articulate as that of Farrokhzad ever existed in Iran, you can come away thinking that contemporary Iranian culture "denie[s] any merit to literary works" (RLT, 25), and that the author's students are "the unlikeliest of readers" of Nabokov (RLT, 22). Neither would the book clarify that living in the immediate aftermath of a revolution and a war might explain the shifting of attention in the 1980s to matters more pressing than literature.

The affection extended to poets in Iran is lavished on foreign authors as well. In fact, Iranians are great fans of good translation. During visits to Iran, I look for newly translated works of literature and names of new translators among the rising stars. In 1986 I had barely finished absorbing all the pleasure of Umberto Eco's *The Name of the Rose* in an English translation when I visited bookstores opposite Tehran University. My jaw dropped to see the book sitting on the shelf there, having already been translated into Persian. I did not buy the book, so I cannot comment on how good the translation was, but its existence alone indicated an audience eager to read Eco's master work even in the war-stricken Iran of the late 1980s. This much I can say with certainty. The presence of such translations in Iranian bookstores is testimony to the openness of the readers and their interest in the world. This is a trait that the New Orientalist vision of the Middle East does not acknowledge. In fact, *RLT*'s depiction of Iran portrays a culture unreceptive to books by Western authors.

The examples I have provided demonstrate that cultural commentary demands specificity and contextualization. The timing, reason, and duration of events are crucial factors in understanding them. Censorship of all kinds is undesirable. But there is a difference between banning all Western books and banning the story of the seduction of the underaged Lolita at a time when a revolution has gained momentum through confronting nontraditional values. Readers other than pious Muslims have had difficulty dealing with what Nabokov allows to happen to Lolita. Indeed, what is surprising is the speed with which the revolution opened its doors on Nabokov again by allowing a government-funded agency to publish, in 1994, a book by *RLT*'s author about the controversial Russian writer (*RLT*, 277).

The issue here is that a lack of specificity turns *RLT* into the dark house where the reader has little choice but to feel his or her way around the elephant that is postrevolutionary Iran. The author's living room is, in effect, a window into this inaccessible world of "oppression" and "religious extremism." In this unsafe and uncertain world, figures such as Yassi, the student who "does not have a private corner in which to think," can be viewed as the epitome of contemporary Iranian girlhood (*RLT*, 32). There are other examples: take the eccentric Tehran University professor who puts literary matters to a vote in his class and expels students who vote against his ideas (*RLT*, 69). It would be natural for the reader to think that with such despots as professors (and even more despotic parents), young girls such as Yassi are deprived of the opportunity to think. To those of us who travel to Iran and come into contact with young Iranian men and women, however, the elephant looks very different. These young people are every bit as intelligent and dynamic as their counterparts anywhere in the world. The same is true of Iranian educators, whom I celebrate in honor of my middle school physics teacher. He used the last five minutes of every class to help us step out of physics problems and into the world. He fostered discussion, valued our opinions, and gave us each a gift that we carry to this day: the desire to look for candles no matter where they might be.

When I entered high school, I chose literature as the focus of my studies. By then, the study of literature was losing ground to pure sciences, engineering, and medicine. The disproportionate prestige attached to training as a scientist is pervasive in places other than Iran and is rooted in a vague suspicion that all current problems in the Middle East are caused by the fact that we have remained technologically behind. The feeling is equally strong among Muslim immigrant families in the West. Exasperated by Western "scholarly" studies of the reasons for our lagging behind, we know in our guts that something went wrong for Muslim civilization to have come crashing down after its glory in the Middle Ages. But what was it? The answer has to "make sense" without requiring too much expert investigation. One popular take on the matter is as follows: our emotional (equals religious) side took over and our rational (equals scientific) one was overwhelmed. The opposite happened in Europe, which was lucky—or clever—not to be Muslim. The outcome is expressed in equally simple terms: they became enlightened, and we turned into fundamentalists. This decontextualized and ahistorical tale of our "failure," which always included a healthy dose of shame and self-doubt, has been further seasoned with guilt after 9/11. Perhaps we will never know exactly how we got here, but the easiest way to get out seems to be to produce more physicians, engineers, and computer specialists. I will come back to this essentialist tale of technology worship later when I talk about my uncle the painter. But let me return to the high school days for now.

I remember kind and supportive teachers looking surprised and sorry that I did not choose to study the more prestigious subjects despite the fact that I had the required GPA. More than once it was suggested to me that one could become a physician, do wonders with one's medical expertise, and study literature in one's spare time. In fact, there are a significant number of medical doctors among prominent poets of twentieth-century Iran. Obviously, they did not opt for literature in their formal schooling. For me, these points were irrelevant. One lived in literature, played with literature, worked with literature, studied literature, and spent one's spare time enjoying literature. Fortunately, I had a great supporter in my father, who despite his love for mathematics was also a poetry freak. He did not think it a handicap for me not to become a medical doctor. I also was lucky to have profoundly inspiring literature teachers at my high school. Some were so good that their ideas continued to inspire my work into my college years and beyond. So, unlike Yassi, I had a lot of private space in which to think.

I would like to think that I found my best friend through Farrok-hzad. It was in the early days of September when the Iranian academic year begins. My middle school friends had dispersed into different high schools. I was finding my way around and trying to get an idea of what it meant to study literature as seriously as befitted a high schooler. One day I walked into class after a recess period and found a famous line of Farrokhzad, also the title of one of her last long poems, written on the board: "Let us have faith in the beginning of the cold season." This is a beautifully crafted and complicated poem in which Farrokhzad weaves a tapestry of hope and despair, a mosaic of life. The cold season signals the beginning of the end. The wind is blowing, the winter is coming, and she fears she will never feel warm again. Still, she finds a way of reimagining herself equipped to deal with the approaching harsh season:

> I will abandon all lines
> And the habit of counting with numbers.
> I will leave the geometric confines of shapes
> To roam the sensual expanses of vastness.
>
> I am naked, naked, naked.
> Like silences in between passionate words,
> I am naked.
> And all my wounds have been inflicted by love
> Love, love, love
> This wandering island I have rescued from the storm in the ocean
> And carried thorough volcanic eruptions.
>
> Falling apart was the secret of the unified existence
> Of whose most meager pieces
> A sun was born.

I do not know if at sixteen I understood what exactly that falling apart was. I do not know if I understand it fully now. But the poem was elegant, mysterious, full of wonderful images, and delicious to the tongue. I read these poems to my then-fifty-something father, who was not just literary minded but fully seasoned in traditional Persian poetry. It was a source of great pride for me to have personally converted him into a fan of Far-rokhzad. "The woman is a grand poet," he would exclaim simply. And I knew that he would not bestow that title easily on anyone. On that day, one early in my high school career, when I walked into the classroom and saw the title of this poem written on the board, I knew that there was at least one person in the room I wanted to become friends with. And I was right — the blackboard writer became my best friend, Zohreh, who carried Farrokhzad's latest collection of poems, *Another Birth*, as reverently as some people carried a holy book.

In Iran, we seem to have a hard time leaving the public alone. There is always something that needs to be blown through a big trumpet so everyone hears it every minute of every day of their lives. In the days when Farrokhzad had introduced Zohreh and me to each other, what Iranians needed to be reminded of was the great glory of our pre-Islamic civilization. Never mind the fact that we had attacked a few neighbors in our day and burned a few places. Those things were a side effect of greatness. We had done much good. Apparently, we had had post offices when no one else had; we had minted coins before others had thought of the idea; and Cyrus the Great had freed the captive Jews of Babylon, which meant we were genetically purified of racial prejudice forever. What is more, we were destined to recover all that forgotten glory in the twentieth century. Well, Zohreh and I did not have any grand plots for toppling the monarchy but loved the way in which Farrokhzad took the wind out of this inflated self-image. All she wanted was to be left alone to remain a simple Iranian citizen and share the normal honors and shames that came with being a member of the human race. She refused to swallow the national rhetoric of self-worship. What is more, she had the guts to say it out loud with the biting humor that came with conviction. In a poem called "The Bejeweled Land" she lashed out at the state propaganda machine:

> O, how comfortable I am
> In the loving arms of the motherland!
> The pacifier of the glorious historical past
> The lullaby of civilization and culture
> And the rattling noise of the ratchet of law
> O, how comfortable I am!

In this infantile state of induced "happiness," the resident of the Bejeweled Land incidentally recognized everything that was wrong with the country of the roses and nightingales. Interestingly, this observer did not think that our most serious problem was that we did not have enough doctors or had not built enough factories. Of course, she did not oppose technological progress. But what horrified her most was rampant consumerism and the capacity we showed for lying to ourselves. She walked to the window of her apartment in the poem and found a metaphorical pile of rubbish outside rotting in the sun. And who should be scavenging in the garbage but the hypocritical poets searching for the right meter and rhyme. Never mind the garbage row. In the loving arms of the motherland, she could have many privileges, not least smelling the plastic flowers made by Plasco factory, and hoping for luck in the grand lottery on Wednesdays.

As fellow residents of the Bejeweled Land, Zohreh and I did not feel one bit ashamed. We knew that, despite its mocking tone, the poem did not ridicule *us*. It did not show disrespect for real people, those who had the courage to shun the artificially inflated national self-image and remain themselves. Had Farrokhzad not had faith in us, who devoured her every word with curiosity and pleasure, she would not have written and published the poem. She did not speak to the elite but to all of us who cared to hear. The fact that she wrote such poems, at once elegant and passionately critical, for us to read meant that she trusted the humanity left in us with all its natural flaws. No, we were not ashamed. She could not possibly be ridiculing us, because she sensed and trusted the delight with which we embraced her narration of life. The trust was not misplaced either. Before, during, and after the revolution, Farrokhzad's poetry has sold like hot cakes.

And that was yet another source of pride for any noninfantilized human resident of the Bejeweled Land. As far as we were concerned, Iran had produced a glorious Eternal Forough capable of voicing our earthly teenage rebellion. Now, a few decades later, close readings of her poems are hard to resist. Good poetry evolves as the reader's understanding of its imagery, theme, and artistry grows with the passage of time. But those were high school days. Our delight was straightforward, as was our fury and rebellion. If we missed her philosophical depth, we tasted the freshness of life in her words like babies who need no training to enjoy tasty, wholesome milk.

At the end of the first year of high school, Zohreh gave me a school picture of herself that I still have. On the back of it is written, "I grafted you on water and on the mirror and did not fear." This was a paraphrase of a famous verse by Farrokhzad, another one of those verses we wanted so badly to understand that we invented a way to do so. I had always known that the note referred to me and to the strength that our mutual friendship gave us. At some later point, it dawned on me that the quote evoked another form of empowerment, too, one that came with having an Eternal Forough of our own. That explains why we returned to some of her poems almost daily. The distinct memory left of each of these readings is a feeling of utter surprise.

Many years later, and many miles away from the Bejeweled Land, when I now talk about Farrokhzad or teach her poetry in my classes in the United States, the same delight and surprise spark the air. Energized by her boldness, everyone in the audience is full of questions. How did she write about those things? Who read her poetry? How did male critics respond to her? What was she like in real life? The questions are endless. Here, I will try to address the one that is most frequently asked. It is a question that mostly puzzles my Western audience but might, in fact, concern those who share my cultural heritage as well, particularly those who nurse a *self* guilty of backwardness. The question is this: how could a person as complicated and open as Farrokhzad be so widely read and appreciated in a country such as Iran, a place with centuries of patriarchy, a relatively high rate of illiteracy, and a deeply traditional culture? To be sure, her main readers are the literate elite. That is true of any poet in any culture. But, as I said earlier, you can pick up a copy of any of her collections, or selections of her work, in a bookstore and find that it is the eighteenth or twentieth edition. None of the editions are likely to appear in less than three to five thousand copies. To this, add the fact that new selections of her work appear on an almost monthly basis. This is a remarkable record, hardly matched by any poet I know of in the so-called developed countries with higher rates of literacy. Indeed, in most cultures that I have visited, reading poetry has been more of an academic and specialized engagement. How can this be explained?

I do not know if I have a full explanation, but I can provide a little anecdote that might shed light on the puzzle. In my last years of college in Shiraz in the late 1970s, I wrote and performed for a daily show on local radio. It was called "On the way to Sundown" and was timed close to sunset. It featured literary and cultural discussions geared toward an interested but general audience. I talked about everything from the book of the year and our notorious Festival of Art, *Jashne honar*, to letters and phone calls from the audience. The show, which I ran for almost three years, aired to about a million people. I was proud of treating the listeners with intellectual respect, never watering down my subjects, as some of my colleagues suggested I do, to make them more "suitable" for radio audiences. I soon found out that that respect was appreciated. In fact, "On the way to Sundown" was once voted the second-most-popular show on local radio. And the listeners often called to share ideas for future shows.

I went on air live for most of my daily forty-five minutes, talking and playing songs or instrumental music in between. But I sometimes also interviewed interesting people, be it a local writer, a musician, a painter who had had a recent show, or an intriguing outsider who happened to be passing through Shiraz. In fact I kept a tape recorder under the front seat of my car in case I happened to run into an interesting person to interview. One day a young man called the studio and asked if I would be interested in hosting someone who knew the entire collection of the poems of Parvin Etesami by heart. Etesami is another major woman poet from twentieth-century Iran, one who has been seriously overshadowed by the grand entrance of the Eternal Forough on the scene of Persian poetry. There is a most unfortunate tendency among critics to put these writers side by side and examine their contrasting traits, which are many. Etesami is more conventional in life and in poetic style but, in my opinion, equally robust and courageous. I had a personal interest in her as well. I had written my B.A. thesis at Shiraz University on the thematic focus of her poetry. Furthermore, I was curious about the gentleman who loved her poems to the extent that he had committed all of them to memory. I told my caller that I would certainly like to meet the gentleman and possibly interview him for the show. He volunteered to bring him over to our studios a few days later. I arranged to meet them a couple of hours before the program. Not everyone was willing to go on air live. Some people preferred to be recorded to feel more control over the process.

I was thoroughly shocked when I entered the room in which my guests were waiting and found next to the young man, who was obviously the caller, a toothless old man in peasant clothing. He was one of those old men who, next to women in black chador, embody the most pervasive visual representation these days of the Muslim world. Except he was by no means dirty or shabby looking. In fact he had taken care to be dressed properly for the occasion. But he was no member of the elite literary intellectuals as I envisioned them. My first thoughts were, "Ok, this afternoon is gone. No goodies for the show. Try at least to have a pleasant conversation."

You have likely guessed what happened: he shocked and surprised me by knowing the poems well, and also realizing why it was important to him to know them. He was happy to go on the air live, and I did a much longer interview with him than I had planned. In fact, he stayed in the studio throughout our day's walk to Sundown. He commented on Etesami's strengths and weaknesses and responded articulately to issues raised by callers. To be sure, some of our theoretical approaches to literature did not coincide, and he understood some of the lines differently than I did. But that was not the point. The point was that an Iranian peasant man born almost at the turn of the twentieth century had valued the poetry of a woman of the era so much that he had become an expert on her all by himself. Well, not quite by himself. At some point on the show I asked him if he could tell us when he had first begun to read Etesami and was puzzled by his answer:

> — No, Ma'am, I didn't read her.
> — You didn't?
> — I can't read, I never went to school.

What? I was flabbergasted, although this revelation fit with his age and background. I asked if he could tell us how he had come across Etesami's poetry then. The pleasure of the memory spilled into his voice as he answered:

> — When I was younger, a literate neighbor of ours used to read the *Shahnameh* and other poems to us regularly. I couldn't wait for when he would read next.

The *Shahnameh*, known in English as *The Book of Kings*, was a popular epic work by the tenth-century Persian poet, Firdowsi. It was common for people to get together and listen to someone reading stories from this book. He continued:

> — Once he read the conversation between the garlic and the onion by Etesami. I kept asking him to read more of her poems every time.
> — Didn't you ever think of learning to read so you could read as much as you wanted?

What a thoughtless question — of course he had! He did not bother to confront me but gently defended himself:

44

— I had a small piece of land to take care of and a family to feed, Ma'am.

And so he considered himself lucky to have had that neighbor and others who could read Etesami to him in their spare time. He could not learn the entire writing system, but he could store what he treasured in his memory.

My audience loved that show, and so did I. And now when I think back on my radio experience, which brought new color and meaning into my then-turbulent life, this episode stands out. I often tell my friends and students about it, though not because I want to idealize the Iranian peasantry or pretend it is okay to remain illiterate. How much more this man could have done had he received proper schooling, I can only guess. Instead, I relate the anecdote because here in the print-dominated Western culture, illiteracy equals ignorance, lack of insight, and lack of refinement. We have an essentialist way of reducing civility and culture to technology and less institutionalized forms of education to savagery and crudeness. It does not even occur to us that there may be cultures in which learning and wisdom are transmitted through channels beyond the written word, or that we have something to learn from these cultures.

The New Orientalist narrative encourages this kind of reductionism by classifying the world into simple and clear categories. There are other uncritical associations, besides illiteracy and crudeness, that lead to similar categorizations. Living in an undemocratic society, for example, is taken as a sign of inferiority and lack of intelligence. "They have lived all their lives in undemocratic systems," we often hear, "so what can they possibly know?" The answer is, very often, a lot. The "logical" conclusion of the reductionist argument is that the poor wretches should be grateful for anything the democratic world cares to give them. Traditional ways of life, falling outside the neat and shining category of "democratic systems," are placed in the large, loose, and convenient bag of "fundamentalism." How could "they" be defined otherwise? No one ever taught them to question things! It is a smug way of looking at the world, not at all pretty and fairly inaccurate. The saddest part is not degrading two-thirds of the world, but the self-deprivation of the one-third that views itself as too superior to learn from traditional societies.

So I keep telling the story of my toothless old man who took it upon himself to carry the entire body of his heroine's poetry as he worked on his land and fed his family. Even the barrier of illiteracy did not stop him. When I met him in his late seventies, he did not drive a car, nor was he rich. But he seemed fulfilled, and in his eyes I could see the glimmer of the simple health

45

that comes with being well nourished. He carried with him his food for thought.

My radio show was a source of fulfillment in part because of my close relationship with the audience, who wrote to me daily. A university professor wanted more discussions of philosophy. A bookseller offered me a special discount because the show encouraged listeners to read. A young girl wanted more of Farrokhzad's poetry. A soldier survived the hardship of military service away from home by listening to my show in the afternoon. I was delighted with the way men and women communicated with me.

Equally exciting was the fact that I had my own crew to work with—the music consultant in the archives, the soundman, the producer, all men well trained in their profession. At first, I did not know how they would feel about a young woman telling them to do certain things differently. In practice, it proved to be not so difficult. Indeed, M., the producer, and I developed a lasting friendship that started with our arguing about the content of each show. I was full of ambition to air my most radical ideas on art and culture. He wanted the program to have something to say to everyone. As time passed our disparate goals for the show got closer.

I remember the day I conducted a live interview with the chancellor of a major university, asking him questions that could lead to political problems for M., myself, and the show as a whole. M. had been doubtful about conducting such a controversial interview from the beginning. I had promised to be careful, but when the red light showed we were on the air all my hesitations disappeared. The sense of freedom and power was exciting. M. would normally watch from behind the glass separating the two parts of the studio. But I did not look at him this time—what if he was either angry or terrified with the bold questions I was asking? The chancellor left as soon as the show ended, and I started looking around to find out where M. was hiding. More accurately, I wanted to know if we were still friends! There was no sign of him. I returned to the studio and threw myself on an armchair we used for resting between air times. A letter from a listener had been sitting on the side table since midday, and I opened it. A young carpenter was returning to school because my show had inspired him to write his own poetry. Wow! Who cared about the outcome of the interview with the chancellor? I read the letter once more then lifted my head and noticed a red reflection in the glass parting the two sections of the studio. A beautiful bouquet of carnations was sitting on the table next to the entrance. It had been placed there when I was reading the letter. The note attached to it said, "Let's have him for a second interview. That is, if he survives this one! You were fabulous."

My radio show came to an abrupt end when I left Iran for England in September 1979 to carry out graduate studies at London University. I lost track of M., who apparently left the country a few months after I did. He and I had been great colleagues and close friends for three years. He knew much about radio work yet respected my unconventional approach to writing and performing the show. Indeed, we had talked about doing an evening show, and I had toyed with the idea of a career in radio. But I wanted to get back to the study of literature and culture. The master's degree I held from Shiraz University was in library and archival studies. Literature was my great love. In addition, I had gone through a malignant divorce about five years earlier following an arranged marriage. I wanted to experience living in another culture and taking a look at life from a different vantage point.

The arranged marriage was not the overdramatized version in which some male member of the family held a gun to my head to make me say yes. I had been born early, at six and a half months. My parents had worried that I would die. My aunt, who had been present at my birth, had said. "she will live to be a healthy young woman and she will marry my son so and so." It was as simple as that. Despite all my intellectual capacity and ambition, it had never occurred to me to question my aunt's projection. Such is the power of accepted tradition in all cultures. The traditions differ but the power remains the same. I stayed married to my cousin for four years and had a beautiful daughter named Atefeh ("affection")," Ati for short. She lives in Chicago now, an accomplished young architect married to another architect. I tried hard to make my marriage work, and failed. The divorce was painful because it hurt all three of us, my cousin, me, and my three-year-old daughter. When I left Iran, I left Ati with my parents, hoping I could bring her over after I settled into my new environment. Little did I know that a war would break out between Iran and Iraq and I would not see my daughter, only eight years old at the time, for another seven years. My parents loved Ati, and my sister Fereshteh, despite her young age, became a surrogate mother to her. But I do not know whether we have recovered — or ever will recover — from this separation.

Divorce was not easy. It brought out all kinds of monsters from the closet of tradition, things very different from the poetry I adored and enjoyed.

There were rules, too, and some quite unforgiving. It very much mattered, now that I had divorced, where I lived, when I came home, and whom I was seen with. This was Iran under the Shah. We had discotheques, for example, yet if I were to be seen there with a young man alone, my insistence on divorce could be "misinterpreted." I was not one to be told what to do. The very literary tradition in which I had been immersed had taught me the value of being myself. Yet it was hard to see my parents worry about my reputation and what it might do to my future.

I don't think I have ever tried as hard to come up with a compromise, something that acknowledged my personhood and my parents' concerns at the same time. Starting the radio show in 1976 was a welcome distraction. Like everything else, it happened very simply. The general manager of the local station attended one of my poetry readings and liked it a lot. An extremely gentle and soft-spoken man, the manager approached me with a job offer right after the reading. I was embarrassed by the compliment and said something silly like, "But I have never spoken on the radio. I can only speak like I do now." He responded, "That is exactly what I am hoping for." With that began a short career that I truly enjoyed. I now had the opportunity to share my jasmine and stars with approximately a million people.

What shielded me from the explosive divorce was my circle of friends. Ironically, Zohreh was not there. She had studied psychology at Tehran University, had married, and was now a high school teacher in Tehran. Our separation lasted many years. We reconnected after I finished my Ph.D. and returned to Iran in 1986. But I had other close friends. Minoo was an oasis of calm, as quiet and solid as a rock. Like Zohreh, she was a classmate from high school days, although we did not share the same passion for poetry. We had plenty of other things to keep us close, not least of which was our independent minds. Minoo later entered Shiraz University like me but majored in history. She was, and still is, the embodiment of the concept of "being there for you." Besides, she could always think clearly no matter what disaster we had to deal with. When divorce-related frustrations drove me up the wall, I would call Minoo to meet. She would simply look at me and ask, "Can you go back and be happy?" No, I couldn't, of that I had no doubts. "Then, better to divorce than to turn into a bitter old married woman," she would say. I agreed. Minoo and I lost track of each other after the revolution but were reunited about five years ago. She was now living in Orange County, California, and was part of a feminist reading group that met monthly to discuss their latest reading. This time, someone had brought a documentary to watch, one made recently about Farrokhzad. As an Iranian literature specialist, I was interviewed for that documentary. "O my God, that's my friend Fati," screamed Minoo. My Eternal Forough had connected me with a friend once more.

I also had another close friend called Zari, tall with soft moonlight skin, slightly curly hair, and beautiful hazel eyes. Zari was a year younger, attended the same high school, and entered Shiraz University a year after me. She majored in literature and, like me, wrote her own poetry. We lost each other after the revolution and were reunited ten years later in a conference hall in San Francisco. I was walking down the hall in the convention center to go to a talk when Zari stepped out of a room. For the next hour we just held hands and walked around the building in silence, aimless and dizzy with joy. Later we found out that little had changed. We could still say to each other in one sentence what we would explain to others in a paragraph. The medieval Persian mystic Rumi once observed, "the Sun is the proof for the Sun." That is, you do not need to point to the sun; it is hard to miss. I will say that about Zari: she is a presence hard to miss. And her presence was another good reason why I did not go to pieces after the divorce—she was there, with friendship, with poetry and all.

One reason why these women were my most formidable support was that divorce brought out issues related to gender and sexuality that resonated with all of them. You could not be a young woman in Iran of the 1970s and ignore these issues. A healthy chunk of the traditional expectations were still firmly in place. The importance of virginity, distinct female and male roles, and the stigma attached to divorce were only a few. Then there was the rhetoric of modernity and change, the mad rush toward technological progress, and the inflated national self-image. Many positive changes had come about. But there was also a feeling that we were on the verge of losing our sense of identity and security. As women, our behavior was perceived as the most precise indicator of societal sanity and morality. If we wore short skirts, the West must be taking over. If we respected traditional family values, all was well.

In the storm of changes that did not always make sense, people like our Eternal Forough were a lighthouse. You could look at her and see that there existed a destination. She had no problem being sexual and in fact had written a few erotic poems that have now become classics. Yet she was not prepared to be anyone's fantasy. She would not sacrifice her intellectual or spiritual aspirations. There was no conflict here as far as she was concerned.

If some inhabitants of the Bejeweled Land got it all wrong, the burden of explanation did not fall on her. She would be the woman, the person, she wanted to be. They could open their eyes to see her for who she was, or close them and sink into their distorted fantasies. At the time, I knew little about the New Orientalist fantasies of Muslim men and women as overly sexual and primitive. We were busy fighting the domestic version, which took quite a bit of energy. Farrokhzad would have been flabbergasted at the mildness of the domestic oversexualization in comparison to the version portrayed in Western popular writing.

The body of popular literature that I critique here provides us with exaggerated and peculiar readings of sexuality in the Muslim Middle East. My specific example, RLT, presents the reader with encounters that often smell of perversion and are tainted with hypocrisy. Human sexuality is complicated and detecting its abuse is a challenge, particularly during times that bring shifts in cultural values. Iranians are not an exception when it comes to abusive human behavior. Nor should writers be expected to cover up such violations. The problem with works in this genre is not that they expose these despicable acts but that they often associate the root causes of these corruptions with the local religion, Islam. RLT places these incidents consistently in the familiar context of the savage, overly sexual, and duplicitous Oriental who in public projects an image of purity and piety. For example, Nassrin, one of the students, remembers a painful incident of abuse at age eleven by a young uncle. In the faint sketch that the book gives us of the abuser's personality and behavior, it is not his sanity or humanity that are questioned. Rather, we read about his tendency to avoid friendship with women as a result of his religious desire to keep himself "pure and chaste" for his future wife. Furthermore, the molestation is carried out during Arabic instruction (further indication of the abuser's religious training). And Nassrin recounts the incident during a conversation about the hypocrisy displayed by "officials and activists in various Muslim associations" (RLT, 48). The reader, predisposed to accept the stereotype of the Muslim male as a sexual oppressor, is unlikely to question the relevance of this individual crime to the overall bankruptcy attributed to Muslim morality. This abusive incident will be just an added "proof" to what the reader already "knows."

The crude and twisted sexual aggression stereotypically attributed to Muslim men and women is usually presented as seeking unnatural outlets.

RLT depicts an example of this while retelling the mourning ceremony for Ayatollah Taleqani. Taleqani, a much respected political figure, died in September 1979. Many, including members of nonreligious factions, viewed him as a force of moderation capable of restraining the revolution from going to extremes. His death, therefore, brought a sadness tinted with fear and uncertainty. RLT describes the chanting, breast beating, and crying for Taleqani not with reference to their exaggerated expression of grief but as "the desperate, orgiastic pleasure of this form of public mourning." The crowd's twisted intention is summed up when the mourning ceremony is depicted as "the one place where people mingled and touched bodies and shared emotions without restraint or guilt." The reader is told of a "wild, sexually flavored frenzy in the air" — "wild," the magical word that captures the crude, primitive, and dangerous all at once (RLT, 90).

Muslim sexuality has intrigued, terrified, and eluded the Western world for a long time. Many European painters, poets, and travelers of respectable repute dedicated large chunks of their lives, and an even larger chunk of their imagination, to envision what it must be like to be under those veils, in those harems, away from the public gaze. Now the harems have, in large part, disappeared, and the veil seems to have acquired a new public/political meaning. Many scholars of the Middle East (themselves of Western or Eastern origin) have interrupted the romantic image of the oppressed female in seclusion by showing that some women might in fact choose to wear the veil. Not only that, these women seem to have a stronger, more articulate voice than quite a few of their unveiled counterparts elsewhere in the world. For the media, however, this image appears to be hard to give up. In fact, my husband and I just discontinued our decade-old subscription to a major national newspaper for this very reason.

I never got a chance to tell you that in 1986 I married again. I married Ahmet Karamustafa, then a Ph.D. student and now a prominent historian of Islam in this country. Ahmet is from Turkey, though you cannot tell that if he speaks Persian to you. I could not have asked for a better companion in life. We have three children: Ati, Ayla, and Ali. I was explaining that Ahmet and I recently stopped subscribing to a major national newspaper because we are tired of finding destitute Iraqi peddler women wrapped in black chadors staring from the front page with angry eyes, clearly not pleased with the presence of the photographer. Or, on other days, it might be a toothless, turbaned old man contemplating a bottle of water as if it had dropped from heaven, or a bare Iraqi body laid on the table to be prepared for the "mysterious" Muslim burial ritual. In today's Iraq, one might ask, are there no young children to be found in a school yard, sitting on a bench chatting and laughing? Are there no young Iraqi men and women looking normal and walking in a park somewhere? I know some. How is it that our well-equipped national papers fail to find them? Or is this because of the war — we are supposed to see the extremes and the exaggerated? The American public is not ever to see, much less know, that the reality beyond our borders might differ from that which the media dares to imagine and show us.

What finally convinced Ahmet and me to discontinue the paper was the front page dedicated to the 2005 Iranian general elections. That page was the last straw. It depicted an entire wall covered with hundreds of little posters of one of the candidates in clerical outfit and a single woman passing by rather closer to the camera than the posters and apparently indifferent to both. Her image was clear enough for the outlines of her face, wrapped in the black chador, to show; yet, her facial features were completely blurred. Was this supposed to be a metaphor for how immaterial women, their rights, and their social roles were to this election? Wrong! Regardless of how each of us feels about the outcome of the election, all candidates had gender issues high on their agenda. Is the photograph meant to say that Iranian women do not participate in elections? Wrong. The candidates, and the women themselves, know how important women have been to every post-1979 election in Iran. Perhaps the front page photo was making a bigger statement about how women are oppressed, marginalized, neglected, and pushed out of the public space in Iran. Wrong again. Iranian women make up 65 to 70 percent of university students, work in all public offices, and play a vital role in the artistic and intellectual life of the country. It would take an entire book to name and briefly describe the women who have made their mark on Persian poetry and fiction, painting, cinema, photography, hiking, biking, car racing, horse riding, music, scholarship, and more. Yes, women would like to reform electoral law and various other legal codes in Iran to get better representation, and, yes, they are still involved in various struggles to improve their lot. But blurred images walking in indifference, they are not. And so Ahmet and I canceled our subscription, having had our fill of toothless old men and indifferent blurred women.

It is not the newspapers alone either, as my delightful friend Alice noted when she and her husband, Frank, joined us for dinner one night. Alice has a Ph.D. in American dance and a deep inner sensitivity in all matters crucial to human beings everywhere. Because she is a dancer, she pays attention to women's bodies and the way they are violated or sensationalized. As we took a short walk in the park across from our house, Alice and I separated from Ahmet and Frank and began our own conversation. "Did I tell you about the program on Iranian women's underwear on NPR the other day?" asks Alice rather shyly. "No," I reply, but the hint is enough for me to guess that our national public radio must have done a feature on the occasion of the Iranian general elections. What subject could be more interesting than women, and in this case they seemed to have selected a very relevant topic.

"You know how sensitive I am to sensationalization of women's bodies and violation of their privacy by talking about things like this," adds Alice. Of course I do. Alice has a naturally beautiful body she takes care of well by dancing, exercise, and good eating. But she is always horrified at women's supposed need for body makeovers if they have a few extra ounces in the wrong place, when the public gaze tells them something is seriously wrong. "The report was about how in rich parts of the country, Iranian women buy very expensive underwear." And she adds her personal commentary: "I think we sometimes try to make the enemy sound like ourselves. It is our way of coming to terms with differences." It is a very interesting observation and her way of saying we are guilty of the same thing ourselves. I tell her I like her observation, then ask, "Don't you think it is utterly and completely baffling that the habit of buying expensive underwear displayed by a few rich Iranian women is deemed suitable for airing on NPR?" Of course she does; that is in part the reason why she is bringing it up. And so I go on. "What is this supposed to say? Look at these hypocritical pious Muslims covering themselves in public. In reality, they are nothing but sex objects to their husbands. They buy the stuff to please men." But don't rich people all over the world do this without defaming their religion and culture? Why does Islam come in every time a weirdo has done something odd or despicable? Alice does not need this lecture; she is only too aware of these short-sighted sensationalizations and media traps.

Worst of all, Alice is right in that an interest in recounting the horrors of Muslim sexuality is spreading. At the more entertaining end, the New Orientalist narrative is importing native voices who can testify to the true wickedness they have personally experienced. As the market shows more and more fascination with the "authenticity" of such experiences, the level of sophistication — and reliability — loses its significance. Instead, observations become more detailed, settings more steamy, and subject matter more closely related to the underwear. With the aid of native writers and what my

historian friend Mohammad would call their "self-orientalizing" tendencies, the new narration puts the European Orientalists of the eighteenth and
nineteenth centuries to shame. It certainly receives more attention and better monetary rewards.

The latest publication in this genre is *The Almond*, "a semi-autobiograph-
ical exploration of sexual freedom" that, according to one of our national
newspapers, "has sold 50,000 copies in France since Editions Plon brought
it out last year. And it has now appeared in eight other languages, including
English." With its frank descriptions of lovemaking, the book has been
compared to Duras's *The Lover* and Millet's confessional essay, *The Sexual
Life of Catherine M*. In other words, take this woman seriously; she is not
just any Muslim woman. But of course, our forty-something North African
author, who goes by the pseudonym Nedjma, has a purpose grander and
nobler than "a desire to titillate." As she said in a recent interview, "by
portraying a woman enjoying the pleasures of the flesh," she wanted to both
"celebrate the body as an expression of life and to strike a blow against the
centuries-old repression of Muslim women." Please feel free not to be surprised. One more defender of the rights of the long-repressed Muslim
woman has entered the scene. And, if possible, remain unsurprised as the
genesis of the book, like many other recent matters, is traced back to the
author's reactions to the horrendous events of September 11, 2001.

As the two fundamentalist camps in the East and the West attack each
other, Nedjma decides to address the "real problem" in the Muslim world,
namely the forbidden topic: sex. Thus, her steamy novel about lovemaking
"is radical. It is a true cry of protest." Lest we mistake this "true cry of
protest" with plain adult literature, we are assured that Nedjma's book is
based on the experiences of aunts, neighbors, and cousins, all women. She
has felt "a moral duty to say: this is what women go through." At the same
time, this defender of suppressed women's bodies apparently does not mind
the sensational image chosen for the book's cover: a woman wrapped in a
shroud-like white cloth that obscures her face and gives the viewer a feeling
that she cannot possibly breathe. Yet, somehow, the cloth is not large
enough to cover her navel. Could this be a hint at belly dancing, meant to
boost the sale of the novel? But of course not. How can a true defender of
abused Muslim women succumb to such commercial motivations?

Sadly, the main problem with the novel is not this charade. Nedjma is
not the first writer to abuse the sexual intrigue associated with the mis-
treated Eastern woman. She will not be the last either. The true evidence of

ignorance begins when our pseudonymous author discusses why she did not write her novel in Arabic. She wrote in French because it felt less shocking to write in a language other than her mother tongue, she explains. But more important, the book would never have been published in Arabic because "it is a thousand years since Muslims have written openly about sex." Well, the illustrious author is ill-informed in her historical observation, if anyone cares to break the news to her. But the true shocker is not her ignorance either. It is the lack of scrutiny by the newspaper that devotes an entire half page to her enlightening discourse on what needs to be changed in the Arab world (no doubt with the help of erotic novels such as hers).

If the newspaper reporter who wrote about the book had taken the trouble to do his homework he would have found numerous Arabic works on sex and sexuality, ranging from purely technical and medical guides, to sociopolitical or ethical approaches, to entertaining Kama Sutras. Had he known this information, he would have asked the author which Arabic language she is talking about. Alas, he did not. The likelihood that she might be questioned on such points by others is slim, too. This is because unlike American, European, or many other kinds of history, for which you need to gain some kind of knowledge and expertise, becoming qualified to write Muslim history is easy. If you have so much as traveled to a Muslim country — even if you did not speak the local language — there is a good chance you can address various aspects of the culture in writing. In the case of native lineage, particularly one not hampered by misplaced sympathies, the odds will improve significantly.

The vast disciplinary domain that in this way opens before you is dazzling. You can be a literature specialist, an historian, an anthropologist, and a political scientist, all in one; and if you are imaginative enough you can invent a few disciplines of your own as well. You are the authority. And so our erotic novelist first displays a genuine interest in theological matters. "It is not the Prophet of God who is responsible for the condition of women today," she exclaims. "It is the Shari'a, the way laws are interpreted, the writings, the clerics who rule Islam in place of God." Fortunately she is antiwar and stops short of suggesting that someone drop a few bombs on them to save the oppressed people. Before we catch our breath, she has turned into a sociologist: "The Arab world is like a sick old man, consumed by gangrene, illiteracy, poverty, dictatorships, fundamentalism." Then she adds a touch of psychology: "Love is only possible when women realize they are not there to be legally raped and men understand that a woman is not a slave or an inferior being." And here comes the personally contributed discipline of psychohistory, presumably based on her observations of people in her native North African hometown. But she makes the statement about the entire Arab world anyway. "The malaise of the Arab world is that people don't know how to love. They watch romantic soap operas on television out of frustration. They dream about love, they listen to songs, they are sentimental, but they are not tender. They appreciate beautiful love poems, but they don't have the courage of the heart." There is little to do except hope that Nedjma's insights in the novel teach us and the inhabitants of "the Arab world" tenderness and clarify such truly complicated concepts as "the courage of the heart."

The barrage can hit you in a single day: NPR's report on Iranian women's expensive underwear, RLT's graphic depiction of a girl's molestation by an abusive Muslim uncle, and finally Nedjma's diagnosis of the sick Arab world. The message can come across unambiguously: Muslims' religious conviction is a big fraud. It is a cover for their crude and abusive sexual behavior. The elephant is so large now that it barely fits in the house.

Some Muslims try to rise to the occasion: "Wait a second, there is a big mistake! There is no connection between teaching Arabic and abusing. This pervert could be teaching anything. Sickness doesn't have a religion. What is going on?" Others prefer the silent response to what feels like living in the midst of a grand conspiracy. The larger public is still waiting outside the house hoping for candles.

It is time for the Eternal Forough to make another grand entrance and infuse the closing pages of this chapter with complexity, tenderness, and hope. That is why she deserves the title "the eternal light." She finds a way to detect the glow of life, so her encounters with others are never devoid of hope.

A poem perfect for the occasion is "Frontier walls," from Farrokhzad's last collection, *Another Birth*. In a sense, this is her poetic manifesto, her philosophy of life. I have chosen this poem so you see her in a poetic instance in which she opens to a range of human experiences: sexual, spiritual, and social. In the light of the candle that she carries, you will see the wholeness of that human experience. At first, Farrokhzad builds walls around a poetically cultivated space vibrating with life. She then turns this space into the sanctuary she desires for all life forms. Within the sanctuary, she takes her readers on a fascinating tour of frozen seasons that come to life with the warmth of love and back to the "fragrant core of a fertilized egg." The poem opens with the building of the basic structures of the sanctuary, the "forbidding walls" that might at first seem to put her in captivity:

> Now forbidding walls
> Rise again in the silent night
> Like plants;
> Guarding the borders of my love's state.

Walls can signify limitation and hide the broader perspective from view. But her approving tone shows that *she* has built the wall to protect her space. The city's "polluted clamor" now moves from her shores, the trees shed their bark, and the earth's pores suck the atoms of the moon.

The fresh air has filtered in through the open windows, the moonlight has cleansed everything and the trees feel safe to disrobe in this nightly perfumed garden. The sanctuary is now hers, and that of all humanity. "Love's longing beat" that spread through her "tribal limbs" is not just an expression of womanhood, but an occasion for the regeneration of all life, for reinvention of the desire to be. This is a sexual and yet intensely sacred moment in which life's perpetual evolution has eradicated all possibility of decay. Farrokhzad expresses the potential sanctity of the moment in which "all stars" are "making love" with the simple assertion that she knows it when it is "time to pray." In this sanctuary, the conventional distinctions between physical and spiritual do not prevail. She now begins to grow and expand beyond the walls. The transformation is personal and at the same time social. In gifting her "young green hot climate's tropic flowers" to the beloved, she is "blown on the last breath of air, through the sanctuary of the night" and rains on all as "madly" as she wants. Clearly, this is not a place to stop, not a place to end explorations. It is the beginning:

> Return with me to that star
> Return with me
> to that star far away
> from the frozen seasons of the earth and its
>   ways to measure and understand
> Where no one fears light

But like all significant journeys, the main move is to cross the inner borders and access the core of life itself. This is where the glow of life can be detected, because artificial compartmentalization has not yet prevailed. This is the place in which the sacred has a vast meaning not yet fragmented with smallness and greed:

> Return with me
> Return with me
> to the start of creation
> to the fragrant core of a fertilized egg
> to the moment I was born from you
> Return with me
> You've left me incomplete

With a refreshingly unabashed tone, she alternates her allusions to light, to prayer, and to the sacredness at the heart of life with descriptions of her physical longing for love. These exquisite descriptions of "doves taking wings" on the tips of her breasts and kisses cocooned in her lips fill the sanctuary with lively and concrete expressions of union. In the last stanza of the poem, she merges the feminine, the natural, and the sacred in the crucible of her poetry then celebrates the alchemical miracle that results. In that sanctuary filled with the moon, beauty may be touched, whether of a single leaf or an elephant. Her unsuppressed feminine voice perpetuates that beauty in poetic articulation. No wonder decay is unimaginable in this garden. The child born here can be Jesus, the one who embodied the miracle of life:

> Let me conceive by the moon in the safety of the night
> Let me be filled
> By fine raindrops;
>   newly beating hearts
> By the weight of unborn infants
> Perhaps my love could be
> The cradle for another Jesus

3

My Uncle the Painter

Once when my uncle was in charge of the army personnel office in Shiraz of the 1960s, an officer walked into his room and approached the desk with a note from an influential superior. He saluted my uncle and said, "I am Colonel X, and this is a note from General Y." The note said the man's business was important and needed urgent — and favorable — attention. This was a common practice known as *towsiyeh*. Often it did not involve a physical bribe. Important people wrote such notes in exchange for favors. Decent people, my uncle included, disliked the practice. He took a look at Colonel X, pointed to the rows of wooden chairs and the people sitting on them waiting to talk to him, and said, "Please take a seat." When Colonel X had done General Y a favor, he had thought he would never wait in lines again, not in the army offices. Surely the head of the personnel office had not paid attention to the note. He saluted my uncle again and repeated, "I am Colonel X, and this is a note from General Y." My uncle looked at him with quiet, unimpressed eyes and said, without a trace of anger or ridicule, "Please take two seats!"

There are so many other stories I could have told you. But this is how I want you to meet my maternal uncle the painter, in his elegant military uniform, completely unimpressed with corrupt power. In fact, many people — including him — wondered how he ended up in the military in the first place. It was one of the ebbs and flows of life, I guess, one that he had been too young to resist. In the Iran of Reza Shah, it had become fashionable for young men to enter the recently established military academy. My great uncle had already graduated from it, and my grandfather on my mother's side had thought it to be the wave of the future, and thus a good route for his son to take. My uncle had complied out of respect for his father, even though he knew early on that his temperament was not that of a military officer.

His temperament was, and still is, that of an artist. He is gentle, extremely polite, humorous, subtle, and yet impatient with mediocrity and corruption. Even in my teen years, and despite the great dignity that Iranian tradition attached to seniority, he would not stay seated when I or any other of his nieces and nephews entered the room. He would rise and show all the courtesy shown normally to a guest his own rank and age. He would not do it as a formality either, but with genuine warmth and a signature smile. We never saw him in shabby clothes. His exceptionally good looks have turned more and more dignified with age. In my visits to his house during my summer trips to Iran, I find him as neatly dressed as he was in my childhood days. Alas, he is too frail now. His hands shake, so he cannot do what he enjoys more than anything in life, painting. He cannot easily cook either. He can no longer make many of the rare dishes he liked to make for me when I visited. They were every bit as artful as his paintings.

Putting paint on the canvas was his great passion. He could lock himself in his studio and paint for days at a time. By some rare turn of luck at the military academy in Shiraz, he had met Mr. Shayesteh, a master painter trained in the style of the most celebrated Iranian painter of recent times, Kamal al-Mulk. My uncle worked with Shayesteh for many years, until the master had given him the classic compliment, "you are now more accomplished than I." He did not particularly like Persian miniature painting. "It is too exaggerated," he once told me. "How can anyone imagine a woman with a waist smaller than her eyebrows?" He was not drawn to modern abstract styles of painting either, though he acknowledged the natural need for change in expressing the creative impulse. Among the European painters he liked were Murillo, Vermeer, Rembrandt, Constable, and Turner in particular. He studied their works and lives with great passion and told the stories of their happy and sad moments as if they were his childhood friends.

Through him I know the story of the little boy who cleaned a studio and secretly worked on some unfinished works of the students at nights. He was later discovered and trained to be the impressive Murillo. I know that Rubens hid behind his larger paintings to hear the uninhibited comments of the people viewing his works. I remember my own gasp with the wonder that comes with sad but beautiful discoveries when my uncle told me, "Saskia was the real sun in Rembrandt's life. He was a master of light and shade, but there are no bright days in his landscapes after her death. From that point on, even the sunshine has a sorrowful yellowish tone with hints of brown." He himself worked with oil on canvas, but watercolor was what he loved most and considered to be his particular strength. In watercolor, he mostly did portraits in a pointillist style that reached back to Kamal al-Mulk. For parts of some paintings, he used a very small brush with only two or three hairs as its tip to make exquisitely small points. Though we have not discussed his reasons for being attracted to this style, I have no doubt that humor has something do with it. He got a kick out of making his biggest artistic statements with the smallest visual signs.

My uncle's humor showed itself in many playful ways. When we were very young, he teased us by putting us on his shoulders and simply walking around. It was a confusing place to be, given the difference in our heights. Later, he would buy a simple postcard and paint one exactly like it. We had to tell which one was the original and which one the copy. He had a stack of them, too. He laughed from the bottom of his heart when we felt just as confused looking at the postcards as we had been looking down from the heights of his shoulders years earlier. In his capacity as head of the personnel office in the Shiraz army, he spent a lot of time solving ordinary problems that could make all the difference in the lives of individuals. He cared to know how much leave time they each had left, where they were stationed, and how they were fed and treated during their military service. Obviously, I did not have many opportunities to observe him in his workplace. The story I told you earlier was just one that many people in the family talked about. On the rare occasions that I had seen him with soldiers and low-ranking officers, they looked at him as if God himself had put a military uniform on to protect their rights. He teased them, too, in his own way. Once, a memo arrived instructing the personnel office to pay each soldier a monthly benefit equivalent to twenty-five dollars per child. A childless soldier, obviously one with little schooling, came to my uncle's office to find out what would happen to soldiers who did not have any children. My uncle announced with a straight face, "They will lose twenty-five dollars for each child they do not have!" Slow to catch the joke, the soldier wondered if my uncle would calculate the number of children he did not have!

I am telling you these little anecdotes from my uncle's life because I want you to see in what way he was as bright as the shiny stars that filled my childhood sky. I would not claim that every uncle or father was like him. In fact, when I was very young, I used to think God must like me a lot for giving me an uncle like that.

In the New Orientalist narration of the Middle East, men like my uncle are almost entirely absent. My specific example, *Reading Lolita in Tehran* (RLT) presents fathers, brothers, and uncles primarily as a menacing group of people. No doubt Iran has its fair share of cruel, unimaginative, sick, or fanatical people. If that were not the case, it would be an unreal country, an invented place, a fantasy. But when you read about the grasshoppers that darken the sky, you should be given a chance to imagine the stars as well. My uncle is a man from that culture, and a permanent star in my sky. No matter where I live, and what I do, that star is going to make me smile and find my way. In the New Orientalist reading of Iran, however, most men have forgotten to smile. In fact, there are few close-ups, candle lights, to let us see their individual faces. What is in sharp relief is the coldness and cruelty of their acts. They seem to do very few ordinary human things like read a funny book, walk in a park, hold a woman's hand, or sit down with her to a cup of tea. Instead they aspire to be a walking harassment with one mission: degrading women.

In *RLT*, most men are like Nassrin's father. Nassrin is the girl who tells the author of being abused by her uncle at a young age. Though not abusive in the same way, her father restricts her movements. Besides a deadly impact on the lives of women relatives, these men have no other personal presence in the book. When Nassrin talks about her father to members of the reading group, she has a detached tone. Not only does she not give any personal description of him, she talks about him with the indifference of an unsympathetic critic analyzing someone's social behavior. She tells the group her "very liberal" grandfather (his liberal attitude is evidenced by sending his daughter to an American school) hired her dad as a tutor because her mom was terrible in math and science. "But then what did she do?" Nassrin asks disdainfully. "She fell in love with my father, her tutor" (*RLT*, 53).

Nassrin explains to the group that her grandparents had considered her father "safe" because of his religious background. But he disproves the assumption by marrying their daughter. It is not clear why Nassrin feels her father's act of marrying her mother is a betrayal of her and her family as well as his own religious conviction. Furthermore, we are not told why Nassrin's mother never sees her American school friends again after the marriage. But we know that, like many other terrible things in the book, this losing touch with the "liberal" world has something to do with the father's cruelty, which is rooted in his religious upbringing. The book gives us at least inklings of the humanity of Nassrin's mom. She "talks about her American school," cooks her family fancy French food, and teaches her daughters English, which Nassrin judges as "rather strange for a Muslim woman." This last comment ought to be shocking to a reading group consisting of Muslim women who read and discuss English literature. RLT is peppered with such incidental comments that suggest to the reader how to imagine Muslim women. More to the point I was making, unlike Nassrin's mother, her father is not introduced with any such personal details. He remains a vague, brute force. In the house, everything goes according to his dictates with the exception of one "concession," letting the mother make the family "weird" food. Even then, this person who once taught math and science is not able to differentiate between the dishes that he lumps under the term "French" food (RLT, 54).

There are other strange things. For example, Nassrin is convinced of her mother's sexual repression and tells the crowd in the reading group she wishes her mom "would commit adultery or something" (RLT, 54). Even in the absence of daughterly affection for the father, it ought to be traumatic for a daughter to imagine her mother in an adulterous relationship. She might as well be talking about her mother and a tutor that she never met. We do not even get an indirect quote from this Muslim villain. Speaking of her father's family, instead of "dad," "grandma," or "aunt," which a girl in Nassrin's situation would use, she speaks of the man "whose sisters and mother all wore the chador" (RLT, 53). Passed through the New Orientalist filter, Nassrin's voice loses all personal associations with the father and reaches us as statements of disdain for Muslim men.

What I am about to say may come as a shock. I can easily describe my often-smiling uncle, and many other fantastic people I know from my life in Iran, as religious. My uncle will tell you himself that his greatest, most fundamental, and most enduring gift is not his talent for painting. It is his love for God. This is a version of love that includes all life. And yes, it is rooted unambiguously in religion. True, it does not manifest itself in an overemphasis on fasting, prayer, and other forms of ritual observation. But it would be wrong to think for one instant that he does not respect or observe rituals. In fact, he still would not miss a single daily prayer at the age of eighty-five. My uncle is very much a Muslim. He believes in the human ability to make direct contact with God and in looking for the inner meanings of things rather than obsessing with their thin surface. Acts of worship are therefore a means for getting somewhere. They are not ends in themselves.

In my uncle's cosmos, angels worship God in the most immaculate way. They are subtle and exalted beings. Angels, however, do not know the emotion of love. God had to create some other being because the angelic acts of worship, despite their beauty and purity, were not enough. God knows and values the emotion of love and does not want obedient slaves only (although obedience is important). He went ahead and designed the argumentative, arrogant, forgetful, and hardheaded human beings who, despite all of this, have, according to the Qur'anic story of creation, a status above that of the angels. The superiority is not out of place. The Almighty put a lot of work into their creation. He molded Adam's clay with His own hands and then breathed into him of His own soul. That soul is, according to my uncle, the ability to love. Human superiority over the angels is for one reason, and one reason alone. Humans are capable of love. You are now wondering, "What about Eve? Why was all the attention lavished on Adam?" You must know that the Qur'anic designation *Adam* does not refer to the male gender but to all humanity. In case the term might be misread — and at times it has been — the Muslim scripture makes a clear statement in this particular case. It proclaims men and women to have been created from a single soul.

Like all accounts of the human journey toward evolution, the Islamic version is not simple. It does not feature the concept of the original sin, but it has other twists and turns in the road. We do not come into this world having actualized our potential to love and fly to the heavens. Love, which is at the core of our existence, can remain inaccessible to us because of distractions such as worldly attachments, hypocrisy, greed, impatience, and taking our own abilities too seriously. Another natural tendency we have is to fall prey to habits and customs, causing us to lose our invaluable urge to seek and explore. That is why Muslim spiritual masters often gave their young followers shocking instructions such as "give away all the valuable possessions you have!" or, "stand in the market place this coming Friday and beg!" To our modern and individualistic logic, some of these instructions sound outrageous. To the masters who gave them, habitual blindness, sleep-inducing comfort, and self-delusion were more outrageous because they meant a waste of human potential.

Once, when a crowd had gathered to welcome the celebrated Sufi of Khurasan Bayazid, the story goes, he took a piece of bread out of his pocket and started eating. It was the month of Ramadan, a time when everyone was expected to fast. According to the story, the disappointed crowd dispersed at once. Whether the story is true or not, it makes an important point. You must rescue yourself from the need for other people's approval before you can see your true significance in the bigger picture. Breaking his fast, Bayazid displayed the fragility of the public image and importance of seeing the bigger picture. With a simple move, he provided access to a new and different vantage point. I am convinced that most of my uncle's jokes, his lively religious practice, and his persistence in putting the fine watercolor points on paper serve the same purpose. He keeps awake, and keeps exploring in hope of finding new vantage points. If we seek, even if we all seek together, we will still find different and separate vantage points. Our corners will be different from one another, and none large enough to house the truth in its entirety. I know for sure that my uncle's is not the self-righteous, serious, and exclusive corner of certitude. He has told me so more than once, from the time I was very young.

There is one instance I remember very clearly. It was a late summer afternoon. We were all in my aunt's house on Nader Street. It was common to visit relatives during the summers and sit on wooden chairs out in the courtyard next to the pond. On those occasions, lots of tea and fresh fruits would be consumed and many words exchanged. How I prefer that to turning into individual silent spots stationed in front of a noisy television! These occasions were particularly good for kids. The younger offspring would run around while the relatively older ones joined the grown-ups in eating and talking. The occasion I speak of was a rather large family gathering at which two relatives had started a passionate discussion over the recent death of a dear friend. He had, apparently, been a respected member of the Shiraz Baha'i community, the religion that views itself as a natural, perfected, and final state of Islam. Muslims, on the other hand, consider Prophet Mohammad as the last of the prophets. That means no religion is expected to follow Islam. For this reason, tension has always existed between the Iranian Muslim and Baha'i communities. These tensions came to a head with the 1979 revolution, during which the Iranian Baha'is were perceived as supporters of the monarchy. Their faith was denied the status of an official religion, and they suffered serious persecution.

The gathering I recall took place well over a decade before the revolution. The deceased was apparently a very good person but "unfortunately" a Baha'i. What would be the verdict now? Would someone like him be forgiven for the transgression of abandoning Islam because of the good quality of his acts? I was barely ten years old and listening with concern as two relatives argued with passion for and against allowing his soul to enter paradise. My uncle had been busy peeling and cutting a peach, which he usually did with a great deal of concentration. (My father always said to him, "It's not fair. I never eat a peach in public because I need a shower afterwards. You make an artistic display out of it!") He had remained busy with the perfect summer peach and had not entered the debate to which he was listening with clear amusement. Only in rare cases would he get involved, and even then he usually exited quickly with a laugh. That day, he must have sensed the confusion that I felt inside, because he said with a smile, as he bent over to offer me a piece of his peach, "Fortunately, our closet is not large enough to keep God locked up inside." I do not think I understood all of what the joke meant at the time. But I understood that the deceased might be entitled to whatever good came with access to our God. I never forget the sense of relief that came with that piece of peach. So, the man was all right. All that he had done would not go to complete waste because he happened to be in the "wrong" religion.

This also marked the beginning of my desire to find that place in which humanity becomes a single community defined by suffering, the desire to be happy, and the struggle to make sense of life. As I grew older, my poets picked up where my uncle had left off. They taught me that humanity is that rare country in which angelic beauty mingles with monstrous flaws in every one of us. I realized how short the distance between the two was. I also realized why laughing was so important to my uncle. He teased us, and himself, because taking ourselves too seriously shielded us from our humanity and the need for finding new vantage points. Laughter, on the other hand, made us all human.

And so, the most shocking facet of the New Orientalist narrative is not its focus on villains of Mr. Bahri's nature, the Muslim student showcased in *RLT* for his quiet but unshakeable brutality. More frightening is the totalizing effect of this focus. It gives men of Mr. Bahri's type a level of supremacy that makes loving male family members, teachers, cousins, neighbors, or colleagues invisible, unimaginable to the point that the reader does not even think to ask, "Where are they?" The chapter that you are reading, then, is my brief counter-Orientalist narration of decent Iranian manhood, and it is dedicated to my uncle. It may be summed up as follows:

Those men without laughter found in large numbers in books such *RLT*, the "serious"-looking truth seekers whose God is small enough to fit in their closets, they cannot mask you from view. You exist, and those men are aliens in your world. Despite being Iranian and Muslim, they are aliens in your world and in the world of many like you. Not so with Laurel and Hardy, who are neither Muslim nor Iranian. I write this in honor of the day you said "They are bound to be good people" to young Ati, who had enjoyed their shows on TV. Then you added as if talking to yourself, "Being able to make others laugh is a gift from God."

✻ My uncle's openness, his ability to empathize with those whose beliefs and practices differ from his own, is not just a fluke of history, a kind of mutation in the Persian cultural evolution. It is not his personal invention either. As Charles Darwin once poetically declared of his scientific achievements: he could see far because he was standing on the shoulders of giants.

Attar of Nishabur, the poet, pharmacist/physician, and hagiographer who lived in Iran during the thirteenth century, was one such giant. Attar could not have lived in a more turbulent time. To his west, in and around the Mediterranean, the Crusades were raging. A group of Christian warriors sought salvation in recovering parts of the kingdom of Christ — though Christ had never preached war in his life — from the undeserving Saracens, who now controlled a good deal of it. Horror stories, ranging from killing and destruction by the Crusaders to burning young boys at the stake, were circulating (although, mercifully, no one could read the detailed reports of embedded journalists on-line the next day while the bodies were still warm). To Attar's east and north another storm was raging, that of the Central Asian nomads headed by Genghis Khan. This latter storm was not quite unprovoked. The Khan had sent emissaries to the court of Khwarazm Shah, a king who ruled over territories that are today mostly in northern and central Iran. The envoys had come in the hope of establishing contact, and none had returned alive to tell Genghis Khan what happened. He had not liked this outcome and was now visiting the region himself, with a sizable army. Apparently, he believed in setting persuasive examples in areas conquered first so those next in line would behave themselves. Things in his wake simply vanished out of existence. Nishabur was on the front line. When the city was sacked by the Khan's army, Attar was killed.

Though this might come as a shock, in the midst of all the killing and turbulence, a good deal of which was fueled by religious difference, Attar managed to believe that non-Muslims were not evil people. By non-Muslims, I do not mean only Christians and Jews. These groups were known as "people of the book," and the Qur'an had already declared that they could go to paradise if they lived a righteous life. Attar went a step further: he believed that every human being — even those not following Judaism, Christianity, or Islam — had something to say and that God was prepared to listen to it. I first heard about this at a young age when my uncle told me the story of

Gabriel as related by Attar. Here is a short synopsis without the metaphorical allusions and elegant imagery that Attar supplies in the original Persian of his classic mystical tale, *The Conference of the Birds*.

One night Gabriel was near God's chamber. The archangel heard the Lord responding to someone, "yes, yes." "I wonder who is calling Him," Gabriel thought. He paid a quick visit to the earth and inspected the lands and the seas but could not find anyone calling unto God. As he returned to God's abode, the Almighty was still responding to the anonymous caller. Gabriel decided he had not looked carefully enough. He turned around and made yet another effort to find the worshiper whose prayers were heard by God. He looked in all the usual places of worship around the world one more time. Since the second search was equally unsuccessful, Gabriel went to God and asked if the Lord would kindly provide directions to the pious individual's whereabouts. God told him to go to a certain obscure temple in Anatolia and look inside. Gabriel did so, and sure enough found a man prostrating himself in front of an idol. He was praying to an object he had carved with his own hands. The angel rushed back to God and said, "I don't understand. This man is not praying to You! He is talking to his idol. Why are You answering him?" God's reply to Gabriel is not just an answer but a lesson. He said, "Just because this man does not know the right way to me, it does not mean that I — who know better — should not find my way to him."

Even at my young age, I was astounded. How could God respond to an idol worshiper? The answer, my uncle explained, is that the purity of intention matters more than the style of worship. Later, when I was able to read Attar's text myself, I felt that in the conclusion to the story Attar wants us to see that "standard rules of piety" are not the only way to connect with God. If you have nothing to offer, he tells his reader in the end, do not turn away. Bring your nothing, for God likes the gift of humility.

A few decades later, Rumi, the mystic Persian poet who has made it big around the globe these days, took the idea and put a clear theological bent on it. In Rumi's version, a simple shepherd talked to God as if the Almighty were another shepherd visiting his house. Moses overheard the prayer and admonished the man for his inappropriate way of conversing with the Lord. The brokenhearted shepherd stopped praying. Moses thought he had fulfilled his prophetic mission; God, however, did not agree. He admonished Moses not to be concerned with the words or the manner of prayer because what really matters is to stay *connected*. In conclusion, God says to Moses, who here symbolizes all prophets, "You have come in order to connect." This prophetic mission statement is so well known among Persian speakers that the verse has now turned into a proverb. If you display kindness in an antagonistic situation, someone present will give you a smile and a compliment fit for prophets: "You have come in order to connect."

Obviously not all Iranians or Muslims share the openness and clarity of vision that Attar and Rumi display. Cultures do not produce giants only. But it is true that many like Attar and Rumi existed, and continue to exist, in the religious culture that these two thinkers represent. This is why the vision of these masters has been cherished and carried forth to our times. How else would my uncle learn to stand on their shoulders and allow his God to grow bigger than his personal closet?

When I was finally old enough to study Attar's *Conference of the Birds* in some depth, I found this to be the main vision of the work. You can sum up the message of the tale as follows: you cannot adopt a religion wholesale and a neatly packaged God along with it. You have to piece your deity together and do it step by step as you grow. Like the birds in the story who seek their king (a metaphor for the Truth/God), you have to seek the Truth during the journey that is your life by building on the smallest moments of manifestation that you personally uncover. That is why, at the end of their journey, the birds find a mirrorlike presence that alternates between reflecting their image and that of their luminous king. Their God resembles them closely.

The bigger tragedy is not that all people of Attar's time were not like him. It is that we, residents of the Western Hemisphere of the globe in the twenty-first century, have made a habit of not seeing giants like him but focus instead on runts. Neither do we always pay attention to the bigger picture of our own lives. We are too busy. Knowledge is now understood almost exclusively in terms of scientific discoveries. Progress is the physical convenience and comfort provided by technological advancement resulting from these discoveries and by consumption. So we reward scientists who give us the theoretical foundation for building things, engineers who translate these theories into actual tools, and business specialists who tell us how to sell what has been made. Aches and pains are not nice and also stand in the way of successful commerce and pleasurable consumption. So we reward our physicians who can reduce those pains and who might possibly find a cure for aging as well. Ironically, the more we make, own, and consume, the smaller we get. And since small people fight easily over who owns what, we reward our lawyers, too. Someone has to decide the winner at the end of each round.

In this scheme of things, mystery equals ignorance. We understand moving forward in terms of the power to open up, unravel, and demystify. Allowing the mystery to take us over is frightening because it implies a loss of control. Experiencing bewilderment, and allowing oneself to live with it, is not a part of our intellectual mind set. This belongs to the "weird" New Age environment complete with the luxury of elitist and exclusive retreats more costly than five-star hotels. God has been conveniently banished from the academy. Credible academics are to keep altogether aloof on the subject unless they are interested in dissecting the Divine that comes with the express agreement that death has occurred. And so a very large number of us live without ever meeting giants like Attar, much less his high-flying birds on their quest for the elusive king. Who has the time? If we had the time, we would see that allowing oneself to be perplexed is in fact the point of the story. The king is naught but an enigma that the birds have to grapple with. Is it a product of their thoughts and actions? Are they themselves the king? Are they themselves, as well as the king? It does not matter. The treasure they will own forever is the journey made possible by the lure of the enigma. You see how hard it is to leave the birds behind. Still, let us return to the concern I started to share with you.

In what way is the perspective that I describe as the New Orientalist narrative implicated in the world's ignorance concerning such bright stars as Attar and his birds? I have already written about the emphasis that works such as *RLT* place on the villains who mask ordinary people from view. But that is not all. Besides the menacing villains they present to the reader, these works carry a powerful damaging subtext, a testimony to a fundamental corruption in the culture. In this narration, all good things in the Muslim Middle East belong to the past. For in their current state these societies have been disembodied of their treasures, which have been replaced with unrelenting religious fanaticism. In other words, all that are left in the culture that once produced giants such as Attar are domineering runts and marauding grasshoppers. *RLT*'s view of Persian literature is both revealing and typical. It does acknowledge that stars such as Attar shone once upon a time; but they are a thing of the past. "There was such a teasing, playful quality to their words, such joy in the power of language to delight and astonish," the book says of Rumi, Hafez, and Attar. But then — poof! — they have all disappeared. "I kept wondering: when did we lose that quality?" (*RLT*, 172) The author thus concludes her discussion of classic Persian literary masterpieces. The answer is rather simple, we have not lost them.

Modern counterparts of Attar are very much present in contemporary Iran. They are lost on authors who do not know the subject well or choose a dismissive attitude toward contemporary Persian culture.

The dismissive inaccuracy does not impact those who carefully follow the developments in Persian literature as reflected in new studies and translations. These studies and translations testify to the superb quality of contemporary Persian poetry and prose that is becoming known to readers across the globe. But such expert readers are few. Those most affected by the New Orientalist perspective are the vast readership whose expertise is in areas other than Persian literature. If you are among such readers, you might never have had the opportunity to meet the Eternal Forough, whom I introduced in the previous chapter. In that case, coming across the mournful announcement of the death of Persian literature is, for you, the end of the story. You will never imagine that such a bright star—with a voice so frank, lively, and humorous—lived right in the middle of the twentieth century in Iran. Instead, you will accept the pronouncement that all the "ability to tease and make light of life through poetry" in Persian culture has now come to an end. The mass media enforces this simplified image on a daily basis: in that part of the world, all that people do is to pray, suppress women, and grow angry at the West. In a superficial and immediate sense, this might even bring something of a relief to the general reader. "Hah! Look how little they achieved after all that American bashing, hostage taking, and flag burning!" But the majority of the readership wants the full picture, it wants more than instant gratification. Not to mention that eliminating lively and moderate voices in representations of the Muslim Middle East serves another equally unfortunate purpose. It gives the extremist stance a major boost by presenting it as the dominant and sustained voice of the majority rather than a short-lived aberration.

The approach to the Eastern Hemisphere as great in the past and ignorant/dangerous at present is a perspective with significant social, political, and even military implications. At a personal level, it can be equally powerful in bringing confusion and discomfort to many communities. I am actually aware of one group particularly vulnerable to the New Orientalist declaration of the death of culture and literature in contemporary Iran. This is the community to which I personally belong, that of Iranian Americans. The impact of this powerful narrative on most of us is such that the deepened sense of shame and guilt can be felt even in brief social encounters.

Most of us were born in Iran, lived a part of our lives there, and/or have family members still residing there. We are a large and vibrant community that promises to make its mark on the future of America. For now, this community is young, full of the drive to actualize its dreams, and very vulnerable. A large number of us speak Persian well and travel to Iran from time to time. Many of us specialize in scientific and technological disciplines, a fact that means we are not necessarily well informed concerning the stars versus the grasshoppers in our own cultural heritage. Nor are we immune to the crude stereotyping of ourselves propagated by the New Orientalist narrative and echoed by the general media. When we think about our relatives, individuals we ourselves know over there, it is easier not to fall for the stereotypes. But when matters become vague and general, we are affected by the atmosphere of mistrust and ambivalence toward *them*.

By virtue of being members of a minority community, we are somewhat better informed about unjust social and political conditions around the planet and the many open wounds left bleeding (this includes the Palestinian-Israeli, Kashmiri-Indian, and Chechnyan-Russian conflicts). And yet, in the tense post-9/11 atmosphere, we find it very hard to voice the desire to move our social and political concerns to the center of public discourse. And who can blame us? We stand a mere inch away from being perceived as accomplices in crimes against humanity. Why make a display of ourselves and risk the disappearance of our small buffer zone? Books such as RLT confirm our suspicion that something *is* seriously wrong with us. Had we not come from the culture of mean-spirited runts and nasty grasshoppers, we could object to certain misperceptions and unjust practices. As it is, we better keep out of trouble and stay focused on things that each of us personally does well. There is no shortage of talent and skill in our community. Besides, why dig deeper when the culprit is most probably among ourselves?

So, as members of the Iranian American immigrant community here in the United States, we are not quite sure where to place our modern educated selves in relation to our part-impressive, part-shameful cultural heritage. In our search for an explanation, we have developed theories that have jelled into grand narratives to help with the sense of confusion. These theories are varied but do have a few things in common. They depend on binary oppositions and sweeping judgments. In their exaggerated black-and-white depiction of our condition, they pay little heed to actual historical details. It is easier to have some explanation for the daily blame one receives, even if it is not a fully investigated answer. Besides, after one grows accustomed to clear-cut binary oppositions, they cease to look coarse and inadequate. Bothersome details have a way of vanishing before the untrained eye.

Please do not misunderstand me, most Iranian Americans generally are not naive or indifferent to details. Many of us are highly accomplished, and our accomplishments routinely depend on understanding the significance of details. Struggling with the impossible, however, can become exhausting, which makes it difficult not to surrender to the images bombarding us every hour of the day. Theories based on binary opposition can restore a sense of order to the chaos caused by these public images. In a sense, these are attempts to understand what went wrong. Let me give you an example of such a theory discussed at parties and social gatherings by many Iranian Americans. It is one of the categorical explanations for things that have gone wrong and is as follows: Muslim religious belief is purportedly in conflict with human rationality and stifles the creative impulse. This seemingly simple explanation has significant implications. Let me explain by giving you a portrait to contemplate, a portrait of my uncle.

It is a midsummer night in Shiraz. My uncle, having just finished the evening prayer, is sitting in front of his prayer rug facing the direction of Mecca. He is neatly dressed, and his silvery hair is combed back. There is a beautifully colored marble rosary in his hand. His eyes are closed, and he seems to be perfectly at peace with himself and the rest of the world. If I share this image with my Iranian American friends and ask who they think this man is, few are likely to guess that he is a retired army officer. If I ask what they think his personality is like, the majority of answers will not include expressions such as "gentle" and "full of humor." If I ask what they think he knows well, even fewer people will think of art history and the German language. If I ask what they think he loves to do most, not many are likely to guess painting. If I ask on what basis they think he makes his life decisions, a large number will choose religious principles as opposed to simple human rationality. Similarly, few people will predict his keen devotion to cooking and love for music.

The sad point here is the simplicity of the reason behind the judgment. The depth and complexity of the person he is has been masked from view by a small piece of cloth, the prayer rug. What has given the prayer rug the uncontested power to limit who he can be is the theory of the binary opposition I mentioned. A person bowing before God is very unlikely to be interesting, humorous, or rational. Neither can he or she have a strong creative self. These qualities are stifled by the Muslim belief. If I told my listening friends that this is my uncle and then enumerated his gifts, there is another easy answer: he is an exception. Not so long ago, in a gathering of Iranian Americans in St. Louis, a prominent geneticist friend put the oppositional theory in clear terms. "It is rather simple," he said. "Once you become a believing Muslim, you have said goodbye to your rationality." Some of us must have looked horrified at the broad nature of the statement because he further clarified, "Well, God is like that red line you cannot cross. He says you have to believe in X, Y, or Z, and that is the end of your personal decision making."

This friend had lived in Iran for a few years after the revolution. His discipline of genetics, to which he was greatly devoted, deals with controversial matters. Some of his professional aspirations were not received favorably by certain clerical figures of a less liberal background. Understandably, this led to frustration on his part. The statement he made about Muslims and rationality was not the first of its kind. The fact that the subject was outside his area of specialty did not trouble him. Naturally one *knows* a certain amount of history, philosophy, religion, and culture. Studying these subjects on a more in-depth basis did not seem to interest him. Yet he once announced, in another social gathering, that Iranians all became hypocrites 1,400 years ago after they were forced to convert to Islam under the threat of the sword. I knew from previous experience that questioning the historical reliability of the mass conversion scenario does not generally yield results. But at least, I thought, his knowledge of genetics might come to the rescue. Could he really, scientifically, believe that a special kind of behavior called "Muslim hypocrisy" had been injected into all of us following the Arab invasion of 1,400 years ago? Would he, as a geneticist, accept that this behavior had then been imprinted on our DNA pattern and carried generation after generation into the present? Well, sure. It was not injected but rather "imposed" as a necessary mechanism for survival, he explained. Iranians had to pretend they were good Muslims, and — since in reality they loathed Islam — the hypocrisy got deeply implanted in them and was passed on to future generations. How else could we explain all the things that went wrong with us after the introduction of Islam?

I will leave the refutation of this troubling theory concerning Iranian Islam-induced hypocrisy for another occasion (although the perception of a mass hypocrisy that calls for a theory is itself troubling). Let us stay with the theme of inherent conflict between the Muslim belief and rationality a while longer. At the cost of stating the obvious, I have to declare to my geneticist friend that his approach to the binary opposition is unscientific and irrational. In his scientific work, he most certainly double checks his findings and assumptions, and the many prestigious grants and honors that he has received to date say as much. With regard to his Muslim faith / rationality opposition however, he sees no reason to test the hypothesis. Were he to read the writings of prominent Muslim thinkers over the ages, he would be thunderstruck by their approach to the matter of human rationality. Take the best-known Muslim theologian of all time, the medieval jurist who has been called the greatest Mohammad after the prophet himself, Abu Hamid Mohammad Ghazali, who died early in the twelfth century. Ghazali wrote with authority on many subjects and taught at the most prestigious university of his time, the Nizamieh in Baghdad. He broached the fascinating subject of the nature, role, and significance of the human faculty of rationality from a variety of angles. I will do away with the technicalities and give you a very brief synopsis of the discussion he provides in his treatise called *The Chamber of Lights*.

Ghazali wrote *The Chamber of Lights* in response to a student friend who requested an interpretation of the famous Qur'anic verse of light (Qur'an, 24: 35). The verse is among the most often quoted and has a complex metaphorical structure adorned with beautiful imagery. It reads, "God is the Light of the heavens and the earth; the likeness of His Light is as a niche wherein is a lamp (the lamp in a glass, the glass as it were a glittering star) kindled from a Blessed Tree, an olive that is neither of the East nor of the West whose oil well nigh would shine, even if no fire touched it; Light upon Light."

Ghazali's entire treatise is focused on this verse alone and places tremendous emphasis on the details. Here I give you the gist of what our Muslim theologian suggests as the interpretation of this verse in the first chapter of *The Chamber of Lights*. Ghazali begins by saying we usually assume that the most important thing that makes seeing possible is the external light that falls on objects. It is true that light is necessary for the act of seeing to take place. However, if our eye is not able to see, no amount of light will enable us to do so. We should therefore understand the Qur'anic concept of light (the metaphor used to describe God) in a more complex sense, according to Ghazali. That is, the concept should include the light falling on an object as well as the seer's ability to see (i.e., healthy eyes). In this respect, we might interpret the presence of the divine in the heavens and on earth not only as the light that is shed on things to make them visible but also as our own ability to see.

He then goes on to say that, despite its vital role, the human physical eye is susceptible to error. It can see an object larger or smaller than it actually is. It can give us erroneous information concerning the distance of objects from us and from one another. Furthermore, our eye will not see an object that is obscured from view by another object. Insofar as our physical eye is prone to so many errors, we have to conclude that it can be a metaphor for the divine light only in the most superficial sense. The true human eye, Ghazali goes on to say, and the one that can learn to correct its own errors, is the rational faculty. It is with our rational faculty that we calculate and learn the correct distance between objects, know the size of things that deceive our physical eye, and remain informed of the presence of an object even though it might be obscured from view. It is, therefore, more accurate to say that when the Qur'an speaks of the divine light, it is referring to the human faculty of rationality.

If my geneticist friend scrutinized his theory of opposition between faith and rationality in light of Ghazali's Qur'anic interpretation in the same way that he reexamines his scientific theories when he comes across a new piece of evidence, he would start revising. I know that if he ever entered Ghazali's *Chamber of Lights*, he would find the excursion astonishing. But sadly, I am almost certain that this exploration will not take place. For one thing, my scientist friend is likely to consider it a waste of time to learn the basic technical vocabulary needed to understand the arguments of the brilliant theologian even if the book were handed to him. And in the unlikely event that he made the effort and understood Ghazali, I suspect he would consider the great theologian an exception to his theory.

Let me make a clarification before we leave our master theologian behind. I am not suggesting here that Ghazali places the power of human rationality above the divine power. No believing Muslim would. But that is where the misunderstanding begins: in looking at the two forces in a solely hierarchical relationship. Ghazali breaks out of this paradigm by viewing the human version of rationality as a ray from the divine light. By so doing, he makes the contest between the two irrelevant and unnecessary. The interpretation can, in fact, be taken to a further, more radical conclusion. Since the human rational faculty is a manifestation of the divine light, putting it to use is absolutely necessary and a form of obedience to God.

The Muslim mystics, the Sufis, have an even more teasing approach to human rationality which they call *'aql*. *'Aql*, as far as they are concerned, is this frowning, conceited authority that knows how to find fault with things and whose presence is absolutely necessary. Alas, it does not know how limited it is. Rumi once told the crowd in one of his sermons that if you wish to make a dress you have to find a good dressmaker. The best thing to do is to use your rational ability to find one in town and then get the directions to his shop. Once you are at the shop, however, the best thing to do is to give the fabric to the dressmaker and let him do the job as best as he knows. The same is true of the journey that is your life. Allow your rationality to find direction to the palace of the king and to lead you there. Once the king has opened the door, however, you must keep this bothersome rationality on a leash and allow the king to work his wonders on you. The king is none other than *ishq*, or "love," the master alchemist who is able to turn the copper of your existence into gold. In a different metaphor, Rumi described *ishq* as the green and luminous emerald with which you can blind the dragon of despair, doubt, and hesitation.

Again, the cosmology that gives clear supremacy to love is not a simple recommendation for the redundancy of human rationality. It has become fashionable to assume that the Sufi path of full trust in God must mean a diminished role for *aql*, which could lead to passivity and complete predetermination. So from time to time, taking the theory of binary opposition a step further, Sufism is mentioned as the true misfortune that led to the downfall of the Muslim civilization. According to this theory, as Europe began discovering the value of rationality and moved outward in search of scientific discoveries, we (whoever the "we" stands for) retreated more and more within and abandoned the quest for learning. The theory concludes that the European move outward led to enlightenment and our inward move led . . . well, every one knows we are not in a good place.

The assumption that Muslim mystics desire a diminished role for *aql* is an oversimplification of an intricate approach to human psychology. Mystics such as Rumi do not suggest that we diminish the centrality of the faculty. Rather, they propose that understanding the limits of rationality is the only guarantee that the tool is used properly. This suggestion applies to using any tool and, in fact, proof of this lies in the instruction manuals that come with simplest appliances we buy for the house.

A more interesting question is why the Sufis give *ishq* such complete supremacy. First, let us get one point clear: *aql* is not an undesirable faculty to be gotten rid of if possible, because if rationality does not find the way to the king's palace, the king cannot work his wonders on the seeker. Second, the Sufis propose that even human rationality itself will not agree with becoming the sole guiding force in the life of an individual. The reason is that we have other strengths that can come into play if we open up the space for them to do so. What is more, some of these strengths are unique to humans. They are a special gift from God. Love is such a unique treasure. In the Qur'anic story of creation even angels, despite the purity of their nature, lack the capability for love. This is what makes human beings the crown of all creation and God's vice-regent on earth. Some thinkers have defined us as animals who can laugh; others have emphasized our tool-making abilities; yet others have said being able to think is the hallmark of our existence. The Muslim mystics say, "I love, therefore I am."

Obviously, diverse communities of Sufis, living in different times and places, do not always espouse exactly the same ideas. But the similarity between their views on many issues is quite astonishing. In a class that I usually teach each fall called "Lyrics of Mystical Love: East and West," we learn that this shared worldview goes way beyond the Muslim tradition and reveals itself among mystical traditions in other faiths as well. For now, though, let us stay with our Sufi's approach to love. Its unquestioned supremacy, according to Muslim mystics, is rooted in an elaborate cosmology. Many of the building blocks used to erect the edifice are Qur'anic edicts. It is not that the Sufis memorized the Qur'an or put it in front of them so they could go step by step according to its rules. Rather, the Sufi approach reflects what certain scholars would call the Qur'anization of the Sufi memory. They immersed themselves in that fountain of inspiration to the point that its words echoed in their personal voices. The Qur'an says that God molded the clay of human beings with his hands and breathed in them of His own soul. God's soul, as we saw earlier, was understood by the Sufis as a metaphor for the ability to love.

The Qur'an also declares that in preeternity God spoke to the seed of Adam, the core essence of all our beings, and asked, "Am I your Lord?" According to Muslim scripture, in that state of preexistential existence, we responded, "Yes!" Sufis label this brief exchange the *covenant*. This is not about sin, obedience, or punishment. It is a promise of love. We fell in love before we were ever born. That is why we were superior to angels even at the point of creation. Still, we have to learn to actualize our ability to love. This requires us to go on a journey of spiritual evolution in the same way that Attar's birds did. Each person's journey entails resting stations and roadblocks unique to that individual. Some journeys require more rituals (fasting, prayer, etc.) than others. All sojourners need peace and justice for themselves and others. Guides are needed for the folks who do not know the way. Those who are more accomplished help others by brightening their paths. In some cases, guidance entails specific and direct instruction from the leader. Very often, however, it comes in a general, undirected way. You have to spot it, reach for it, and put it to use. Rumi once wrote that the greatest masters teach without saying a word. They show you the way by being there. Then he used one of his classic metaphors, packing a remarkable amount of wisdom into a single thought: "If you are lost in the desert, you look at the stars to find your way. Do the stars ever talk to you?" I have always thought of my uncle's painting and his vibrant laughter as a starlike presence, even when I did not know about this elaborate Sufi cosmology of love. My uncle would simply enter the room, and everything would appear in a different light.

So, what is it that King Love can do that Guide Rationality is not able to achieve? To make a very long story short, stubborn, hardheaded devotion comes only with love. Rationality will doubt, calculate, stay away from risk, and keep asking questions. These are all good qualities for finding one's way to the king, for getting there. Once you have arrived, however, you want to get beyond the bickering and taste the union. Would a lover ever need to be persuaded that she or he is in love? She or he knows that with every atom in his or her being. Love will stop talking and seek union. It will go forth in the face of all odds. That is why Rumi describes it as the emerald that will blind the dragon.

Why is such boldness needed in the first place? Because, like Attar's birds, we have to piece together our personal Truth, and that is not simple. Picking a packaged God and bowing before it is easy, but discovering, rather shaping, one's own is not. Furthermore, remember how closely God resembled the birds themselves. That is where the true difficulty lies: what we need to remake and piece together is ourselves. That is where the emerald of *'ishq* comes in handy to deter the dragon of doubt. In his discourses Rumi attempted to explain to the congregation what happens when humans — with all their attachment to small things — come face to face with the vastness of love. He used another metaphor, this time an extended one. When your house is small, so are the number of guests you can entertain, he said. Don't you see that babies only want milk and their mother's love when they are very small? As their bodies grow, the guests of senses, perceptions, and rational thought arrive. These guests continue to grow in number and in complexity until the baby is a fully grown human. Then one day, King Love arrives with a vast army and all the royal belongings. The king takes a look at the house of your being and says, "We cannot possibly fit in here. Let us tear the house down and build a palace!"

You are so delighted with the arrival of the king, being in love, that allowing yourself to be torn down and remade is a small thing to do. What if *'aql* quibbles now and then? You will not even hear it.

My uncle made a difficult decision by listening to *'ishq*, and, it seemed at the time, ignoring the quibbling of *'aql*. In the early 1970s, he decided to retire from the army soon before he was to be promoted to the rank of general. *'Aql*, together with a lot of friends and acquaintances, said this was the wrong choice. He had worked so hard for so many years in the army, it would be self-destructive to retire early when he was just about to be promoted. *'Ishq*, however, reminded my uncle of the grave powers that come with the glory of a high-ranking position, particularly when the authorities at the top may not always be moving in the direction of your choosing. The truth was that the army would have most certainly wanted him in one of its courts because he was deeply trusted by lower-ranking officers and by people who knew him in general. Military courts were not the place he wanted to spend his last working years. He did what *'ishq* suggested, walked away from the promotion and left Tehran, which had been his home for almost two decades.

Within a few years of my uncle's resignation and his return to Shiraz nationwide unrest began. This unrest was manifested at first in sporadic confrontations with the Shah's armed forces and secret police. The regime dismissed these confrontations as isolated terrorist incidents. As they became more prevalent, spreading to university campuses and streets, the government began to describe them as leftist or Muslim/Marxist conspiracies. In reality, leftists, Muslim activists, and the National Front were all joining the opposition. While participants in armed struggle were arrested, jailed, or executed, attempts were also made to alleviate the discontent by introducing minor political reform into the system. Later, when I was in England, I realized that the outside world had not known of the gradual crystallization of these oppositions into a major antimonarchy movement and had been somewhat surprised by the 1979 revolutionary explosion. For those of us who lived in the country, however, the spread of discontent and the unification of oppositional fronts, as well as regular public demonstrations, made the revolution predictable as early as 1978.

When my uncle returned to Shiraz, the unrest had not begun yet. He purchased a small piece of land near the historic Eram garden, in the northern part of the city, and built a house. He would visit us for lunch often because his family had not yet moved to Shiraz, waiting for the construction to be finished. I remember his excitement over the masonry. It was not an overly luxurious house, but it was beautiful. It had a patio with a decorative palm tree in the middle of the hall. He had searched carefully for a stonemason who cared about artistic details. Every day, my uncle spent hours watching the master mason working on the front of the house. Then he would say, "You should come to see him work with his hammer and chisel cutting and shaping the stone. Every square inch is made of so many fine pieces. Usta is a great artist. He really is!" I never went to observe Usta in action, but I had no doubt about his mastery even before I saw the finished product. My uncle would not use the word "artist" lightly. Besides, who cared about the stonemason? I had my star back in Shiraz. My uncle would shine his light in my life again until I left Shiraz for England in 1979. Soon, I would be visiting my uncle's house several times every week, as he would ours. We would read poetry, listen to music, talk about things in general, eat wonderful food; when I was lucky I would catch a glimpse of him working on a painting. Of all the images this one comes to mind most often: I climb up four steps and ring the bell. Shortly after, the polished wooden door cracks open. Then his tall figure and his bright welcoming smile appear in the frame.

My uncle and his wife have since moved back to Tehran, where their daughter and son live with their own families. Shiraz is not the same when I go for visits, but I am glad that he and his wife have their two devoted children to care for them. I had a short and delightful exchange with him a few years ago when he was still in Shiraz during one of my excursions to Iran — always brightened by visits to his house. This is another example of his humor and how much we say to each other in a few words. We can do that because the bigger story has already been told for us. We share that thousand-year-old, thick forest of images and ideas that have grown out of the seeds of thought and play planted by Attar, Rumi, and others. When one of us picks a single leaf, points to a rare bird on a tree, or touches a branch, a song begins to resonate throughout the forest. This one is a memory that will stay with me, like the fragrance of the jasmine wrapped in my grandmother's prayer rug.

It was the late 1990s and a terribly hot summer in Shiraz. Ahmet and I had spent a month selling my parents' old house and buying a smaller place, renovating it, and moving them in. Our aching bodies no longer remembered what had been happening even the day before. All I could feel was that I was tired. It had all been made possible through the generosity of a man in the realtor's office, whom I will call Mr. J. We hardly knew Mr. J. But for reasons unknown to us, he and his family liked us and helped us through the difficult task of moving my parents. Furthermore, this man in his early forties seemed to have experienced all manner of jobs, from photography to selling antique objects to real estate work; he knew his way around all kinds of offices we needed to frequent to get our work done. Friends had suggested that he might be hoping for a monetary reward or favors related to a trip to the United States. As it turned out, however, he wanted nothing in return. He was just a kind person. We continue to visit Mr. J. and his family when we go back to Iran.

Having triumphantly finished all the bureaucratic paperwork regarding the purchase of the house, and having moved my parents into it, I focused on details such as connecting the phone. If you live in the United States, connecting the phone is nothing to write home about. In Iran, it can be an elaborate ritual involving a long wait just getting the new telephone number. We were past that stage now. I was standing in the living room with the phone in one hand and the cord in the other, trying all possible outlets. For one instant I seemed to get a dial tone then lost it. So there was hope. I fiddled around with the plug and tried again. No, it was not working. I was hoping to visit my uncle and his wife for lunch, yet the phone delayed me. Ahmet was taking care of another chore, and Mr. J. had to take a relative to the doctor; I had to do it myself. I plugged the phone in one more time and bingo! There was a dial tone, a stable one. I had not put the receiver down yet when the phone rang. Who knew our phone number? My uncle, of course. I had given it to him myself. I screamed with the joy of having scored a major victory: "I just connected the phone, *Daee Joon* (that's how I address him). I have connected the phone, it works. It works!" His deep voice said with a hint of the familiar laughter from the other end, "You have come in order to connect!"

And I was transported from the hassle of connecting the phone right into the company of Moses.

My uncle used the line from Rumi describing the prophetic mission of Moses to connect God and humanity to demonstrate the significance he attached to my trip from America to take care of my parents and keep them connected to the community. We both knew that the prophetic attribution was a loving stretch of the imagination, meant to express his admiration and gratitude. What made the parallel possible was the fact that Rumi's verse had by now become a proverb that one could apply to ordinary people.

Let me take you from here to a totally different place, one in which communication does not depend on the classic Sufi tales. Neither is poetry the central medium there. This is the novel *Women without Men*, in which Shahrnush Parsipur, who wrote before and after the 1979 revolution, takes contemporary Iranian women on an imaginative journey of self-discovery.

4

Women without Men
Fireworks of the Imagination

She walked off the plane tall and curly haired, slightly agitated, and wearing a half-amused smile. I thought, "So much like her stories!" Shahrnush Parsipur was coming to St. Louis to speak to my class called "Writing and Rebellion: Women Writers of the Near and Far East." I was coteaching the course with two women colleagues, Nancy and Rebecca. Anyway, we had read Parsipur's novel *Women without Men*, and now she was coming to speak to us in person. The last time I had wanted to invite her, she had been in Utah and had returned to Tehran before a trip could be arranged. This time, she was in California and had the time. I welcomed Parsipur to St. Louis and introduced her to my husband. I guess — given the title of her novel — she was a bit amused that the two of us had come to pick her up together. We walked to the luggage area exchanging pleasantries, asking how her time in California had been. "Fairly quiet," she answered in a dreamy voice. Then she turned to both of us rather suddenly, saying, "No one climbs up my window — not a thief, not a lover!" We laughed. She had been so serious it was hard to do anything else. I knew she loved to be surrounded by people. When invited to give a talk she would say, "Just don't throw me into one of those hotel rooms. I don't care about the rest." That is why we had arranged for her to stay with a friend. Now, ten seconds after we had met, she had wrapped the dilemma of her life in a joke and held it in front of our face. And yet her voice was neither disappointed nor bitter. I thought, "So much like her stories."

Surprising. Excited. Fired up. Sometimes even angry. But not bitter. That is how I would describe Parsipur's stories. And of course, brightly imaginative. Nowhere is this better displayed than in her short novel *Women without Men*, published in 1989 in Iran. Why would she be bitter? She has *personally* given herself the "right to free access to imagination," the article that Nafisi wants to add to the Bill of Rights in her "recurring fantasy" in *Reading Lolita in Tehran* (RLT, 338). No, Parsipur's imagination is not a fantasy. It is real. And it is a phenomenon in contemporary Persian fiction.

The blurb on the cover of the English translation of her novel reads: "The significance of Parsipur's work transcends the realm of literary activities. Her works were among the first feminist-conscious enunciations that appeared in the post-revolutionary period in response to limitations imposed on women by the state ideology." It goes on to list other prominent women writers such as Ravanipur, Behbahani, and Danishvar who responded to these limitations with their unmistakable voices, and above all with their lush imaginations and creative energy. These women were armed. The weapon they carried — one that could not be confiscated — was and is their towering presence.

I would slightly rephrase the blurb: while Parsipur's writing pushed strongly against the "limitations imposed on women by the state ideology," the significance of her literary contributions transcends that. In the opening pages of *Women without Men*, we find out that the life of her main protagonist, Mahdukht Parhami, is completely screwed up by the simple yet horrifying trick that the shifting paradigms of the many-faced popular culture have played on her. Mahdukht teaches in a primary school, and Mr. Ehteshami, the principal, fancies her. "Miss Parhami, please put the registry away! Miss Parhami, please ring the bell! Miss Parhami, please say something to the janitor, you understand her better!" One day, Mr. Ehteshami says, "Would you like to go see a movie tonight? There is a good one showing." Mahdukht is angry. What the heck does he think he is doing? What kind of a girl has he taken her for? So that is why everyone has a funny smile when Mr. Ehteshami talks to her! To show him, and the rest of the world, what kind of a person she really is, she does not just refuse the invitation. She quits her job as well. A year later, when Mahdukht hears that Mr. Ehteshami has married Miss Ata'i, the geography teacher, her heart is "leaping out of her chest" with pain. So that is what he meant when he asked her out. The times have changed!

And yet, the biggest trial women face in the deceptively changing world is not to understand what it is that everyone wants from them. The biggest trial is to remain themselves in the midst of the confusion and the chaos. Parsipur's answer, like that of all wonderfully complicated people, is simple and profound at the same time. Hold on to your imagination and get out of the corner that has been "assigned" to you, she would say. It does not matter who has assigned it — religion, society, culture, politics, or yourself. Just get out and take a good look! Remember, you have an imagination that can change your life. Like all important things, this getting out is laden with pain and danger. But how can you know that you will not grow roots and thrive in a garden if you have never planted yourself in the moist earth? Parsipur's short inscription on the first page of my copy of *Women without Men*, a reminder of her brief but memorable visit to St. Louis in 1999, reads, "To dear Fatemeh, in the hope that women set out to discover the world." That is not a casual dedication note. It is Parsipur's literary vocation. Meanwhile, Mahdukht, now a spinster suffocating in Tehran's scourging summers, is about to visit other places. Idiots! They do not understand that these huge windows are not for this kind of weather, she thinks, and accepts her brother's invitation to visit his garden in Karaj, a small town outside Tehran. But there is more going on here, since she is planning to plant herself in the cool moist earth of the garden at the start of the winter. In time, she will become a tree with a thousand branches spreading everywhere. Even Americans will buy some cuts and plant them in California to create a Mahdukht, or Maduk, forest (they will not be able to pronounce her name correctly). The best part is that decades later, linguists will still be confused over her name and biologists over her place of origin. How perfectly delightful! And how impossible to predict what could happen next.

Parsipur has written plenty of fiction, short stories and novels, some of which have already become classics in modern Persian literature. The English translation of *Women without Men* provides a full annotated list of these works. She made a grand debut with the novel *The Dog and the Long Winter* (1974), which was accepted as a serious work of fiction right away. It is about a young woman's fascination with a revolutionary brother and her agony to understand herself as she watches the trials and tribulations leading to his suicide. By the time her other major work, the novel *Tuba and the Meaning of the Night* (1989), was published Parsipur was already a distinguished writer. The protagonist of the novel, Tuba, is from the upper class. Like her counterpart in *The Dog and the Long Winter*, she must explore the pressures and the limitations that come to impose themselves on women universally. What is with this "assigned" place that keeps them from discovering the world? More importantly, how can women break out of it and get on the road?

In *Women without Men*, the protagonists have asked and answered that question. Here, women are stars shooting and firing in all directions. At the same time, they are painfully, and universally, ordinary. The ordinariness they share with each other, and with many women elsewhere in the world, gives them a great power. If they successfully moved out of the places assigned to them to discover the world, so can we. Parsipur, however, does not say that. Preaching is the last thing she will do. We have to do our own excavation in search of such overarching meanings. Besides, the women in the novel have a very ordinary and immediate destination: the small town of Karaj. They all head in that direction and come together in a barely visible yet almost cosmic contraction that directs their journey. Parsipur artfully hides the delicate underlying structure from us and allows it to emerge step by step, like a little surprise, as we get to follow each woman on her way to Karaj and the larger world. Then the group is undone, and the women spread back into the world as if the cosmic force has let go of the stars and they are breaking out of their constellation.

As we discover, step by step, that the women are heading for the same place, we find out that, despite their intriguing differences, they have much in common. These include experiences and feelings but most of all a newly found agency. Parsipur's language is simple, frank, intentionally unrefined in places, and charming in its imperfection. She pulls us in. We are on the road with the women, involved in their adventures and thinking every once in a while, "Aren't I a bit like that?" But first, she takes the time to introduce us to her protagonists. Contrary to the eventful arrivals of the women, which have all the hustle and bustle of a wounded soul's return home, the spreading out is a gentle but assured expansion. The garden in Karaj is a safe haven. The "good gardener," the only man present, is sweet and nurturing. He serves and entertains the women but is not a threat. For the first time in their lives, these women without men are left alone to just be who they are. This is a place in which an ex-prostitute, a woman who has pushed her menacing husband down the stairwell, and a mind reader live together and in safety. Now that they know how to live, they also know how to spread out in the world gently. No need to rush. Let us meet the women in their pre-Karaj surroundings.

Amidst the violent street demonstrations of the 1950s in Tehran, Faizeh is taking a taxi to visit her friend Munis. She risks being killed just so she can at last air her frustration about her sister-in-law, Parvin, who has not been appreciative of her kindness and her cooking. Faizeh has read some-where that round-faced people are stupid. Although Munis does have a round face, she is Faizeh's only hope for a sympathetic ear, and so Faizeh undertakes the visits. The conversation between the girls is rich in cooking details, but the most fascinating part is their argument over what virginity is. Faizeh's sister-in-law has accused her of not being a virgin. Now the girls argue about what virginity really means. One thinks the word refers to a sheet and the other to a hole. This discussion of virginity, responsible for the initial censorship of the book in Iran, is fascinating. The girls are ignorant about something that haunts them in life and categorizes them as decent or indecent. Parsipur does not apologize for women's shortcomings, nor does she hide them. Instead, she holds them right in front of our face. In this case, ignorance is not the worst problem either. Faizeh is petty, scheming, and dishonest. She will do anything to maintain her reputation as a virgin and to get the attention of Amir — Munis's brother — and marry him. That is her ultimate desire. The perilous street fights outside hint at the dangers she will face if she does not have a husband to accompany and protect her. What is more, this husband-to-be prefers innocent and stupid women. When Amir enters the room and notices Faizeh and Munis talking, he asks why they have been crying. Faizeh, anxious to show she is ripe for marriage, gets straight to the point, "Well, we are women."

Unlike Faizeh, Munis is a genuine person. She is, therefore, genuinely offended by being told a lie about virginity. All her life she has refrained from climbing trees for fear that it might damage her virginity. Now it turns out to be a hole! She is so angry that she kills herself, but not by taking sleeping pills or cutting her wrist. No, she jumps off the roof into the perilous street! And because the authority in charge here is Parsipur, not God or men, Munis simply gets up and roams around the streets of Tehran as if she had not died. The first thing she does is buy a book from the bookstore and read about her sexuality. After a month, she is calm, wise, and ready to pick up her life where she left off. She returns home. Amir deplores an independent woman who has been on the street by herself as much as he wants to marry a meek one who would be afraid of going out without him. How can he put up with this blemish on the family's reputation? He kills Munis. Faizeh finds him with the body and helps cover up the crime. Cooperation in murder does not produce the desired outcome. When Faizeh reminds him of his need for a family, Amir agrees and decides to marry a neighbor's eighteen-year-old "pretty, soft, quiet, shy, kind, reserved" daughter.

You might be now wondering why Parsipur's negative characterization of Amir is not in the same category with the vilification of Muslim men I criticize in the New Orientalist narrative. The differences between the two are many and significant enough for us to take a cursory look at a few of them. First, *Women without Men* is fiction with no claim to chronicling historical incidents. Parsipur's teasing tone keeps the fictional nature of the characters in the foreground at all times. Second, her nuanced narration of events allows the reader to feel empathy with people on all sides. The matter under scrutiny in the novel is human frailty and flaw, not a particular ideology, culture, or religion. The reader is, therefore, not encouraged to construct two distinct categories of "us" and "them." Furthermore, Parsipur wrote *Women without Men* shortly after the 1979 Iranian revolution, which was expected to enforce patriarchal habits. She wrote her novel in Persian for the men and women whom the novel fictionalizes as potential agents or targets of patriarchy. Like Farrokhzad's poem "The Bejeweled Land," the novel is an indication of the author's trust in the self-critical ability of the reader and in his or her awareness of the complicated relationship between fiction and truth.

Back to the story, Faizeh is devastated by the news of Amir's marriage to another woman, and Munis returns from her second death, only stronger than before. The first thing she tells Faizeh is that despite her round face, she was never stupid, and the second is that Faizeh should learn to live with her sister-in-law Parvin being a better cook than she. Since this is the night of Amir's wedding, Munis pays a visit to the nuptial chamber to tell Amir that the girl is not actually a virgin but that he will have to live with her without throwing a tantrum or causing any harm to her. So the chapter winds down with the twice-dead Munis telling a terrified Amir that if he lifts a finger to harm his nonvirgin wife, she will be back to give him a lesson. Then, amidst the groom's profuse crying, Munis holds Faizeh's hand and heads out of the house into the dark night: "Come on, Sis!" she says, "Let's go to Karaj."

The fourth woman we meet in the book is Farrukhlaqa. The beautiful, fifty-one-year-old Farrukhlaqa is an attractive upper-class woman. Her husband, Mr. Gulchehreh, is terrified of his love for her. If she finds out how desirable she is, she will never take him seriously. She might even leave. So he spends most of his time teasing her about being badly dressed and getting close to the age of menopause, asking periodically whether he should be thinking about finding a younger woman for himself. He can view her without the anxiety of revealing his true feelings only by looking at her reflection in the mirror. That way he can watch her move around the room while he pretends to shave for a very long time. When they are face to face, all he can do is wear a nasty smile, one that appears to ridicule her.

Really, it is designed to cover up his love and his fear of losing her. Worse still, Gulchehreh has recently retired, so he is at home a lot more, giving Farrukhlaqa no room to breathe.

She has a fantasy, Fakhr al-Din, a friend of the family who leaves for the United States when she is only thirteen. He visits Iran from time to time and, during the last years of World War II, brings his wife and two boys with him. Fakhr al-Din is not just good looking. He treats Farrukhlaqa with respect and tells her she is beautiful every time they see each other in family gatherings, likening her to Vivien Leigh in *Gone with the Wind*. In fact, fantasies about Fakhr al-Din are all that brighten Farrukhlaqa's life. Then the war ends, and Fakhr al-Din takes his wife and children and returns to the United States. As if that was not bad enough, he dies in a car accident. Now that he is dead, the fantasies are not possible any more.

One day Gulchehreh loses his mask of indifference. He is just tired of pretending. Besides, he thinks, now that they have lived together for thirty-two years, and she has reached the age of menopause, perhaps he can show Farrukhlaqa his feelings without "dying for her." He walks toward her, something he has not done in a long time. They come face to face on top of the stairs. He musters courage and looks her right in the face, without the regular nasty smile. As if this act was not strange enough itself to alarm Farrukhlaqa, he calls her name with affection. This can not be, she thinks. He must have something nasty in mind. "What if he kills me?" is the last thing that goes through her mind. She punches him in the stomach and he loses his balance. Her reaction is not like that of Scarlett O'Hara, who got mad when Rhett ridiculed her about her pregnancy. The result of her actions is the opposite of what happens in *Gone with the Wind*, too. Instead of Scarlett, this time Rhett falls down the stairs.

Three months later, Gulchehreh is dead. Farrukhlaqa has sold the house and found a garden, a very green one, located on the bank of a river. Yes, you are right: the river and the garden on its bank are in Karaj.

The next person I would like to introduce you to is Zarrinkulah, the woman whose story is the shortest and most moving of all. She is my favorite character in *Women without Men*. Had I been the author, I might have called the novel *Zarrinkulah*. But you have to wait just a page or two before meeting her. There is something else I have wanted to bring to your attention, something that would not have made much sense until now. I had to assume you have not had much opportunity to read Persian novels.

Now you are familiar, to a degree, with at least one example of the contemporary Persian novel: Parsipur's *Women without Men*. This is not an entirely representative work for the author because it has a strong flavor of magic realism. It is also shorter than her realistic novels mentioned earlier. Still, you can see the variety of voices and the differences in their background, personality, and interests. Even on the basis of this one example I can now explain the point that I have in mind.

Let me put it this way, if you did not have the chance to meet Parsipur — and the women whom she writes about — what I describe as the New Orientalist narrative could convince you that they do not exist. According to this narrative, the undemocratic social conditions prevalent in the Middle East prevent the genre of the novel from flourishing in that part of the world. *RLT*, our example of the New Orientalist narrative, enforces this perspective in relation to Persian culture. The novel's "basically democratic structure," the book tells us, is in conflict with the undemocratic social conditions of Iranian society. On this false premise, it then concludes that the "realistic novel was never truly successful in our country" (*RLT*, 187).

This is not the place to review the colorful history of the novel in Iran. A simple search on the Internet for fiction writers in twentieth-century Iran puts the theory that this literary genre has not flourished in that part of the world to rest. No need to duel on the success of these works. But it is important to examine the nature of the explanation and comment on what has come to be known as the Bakhtinian perception of the novel. The Russian critic Mikhail Bakhtin, and European critics who expanded on his ideas, considered the novel with its multiplicity of voices to be an essentially Western genre, a result of the democratization of social structure. That is why they consider many Eastern cultures to be incapable of making significant contributions to this genre.

This exclusivist outlook was a product of two interrelated conditions, among others. The first was a Eurocentric perception of the world that argued for the centrality and uniqueness of Europe. Postcolonial and subaltern criticisms, developed in the latter part of the twentieth century, have since exposed the limitations of the Eurocentric worldview. Second, until fairly recently, generic studies have been carried out exclusively by literary critics who, despite their impressive knowledge of Western traditions, know little about literature produced in other parts of the world. Making generalizations without having the necessary breadth of knowledge to support them is a characteristic of many canons shaping our views in generic studies.

That is why it is important to learn about major writers such as Parsipur in other traditions. It is the only way to correct the hasty and ill-informed generalizations resulting from the urge to classify literary forms, to give them names, to study their origins, and to understand their influences on one another.

The New Orientalist narrative continues to perpetuate the outmoded Eurocentric approach to the novel. Building on this faulty foundation, RLT adds a number of its own assumptions. First, the book uses the same simplistic method of literary analysis for which it criticizes the Muslim activist bad guys: confusing fiction with real life. In the book, the attitude of male students Nahvi, Nyazi, and Bahri is presented to us as crude, unsophisticated, and politically motivated when they accuse Gatsby of corruption and some women in Austen's or James's novels of frivolity. These students are ridiculed for their inability to separate fact from fiction. At the same time, the book judges the current state of the Persian novel (which it does not examine) to be poor and considers the condition to be the literary implication of reality in Persian society.

Second, from a literary theoretical perspective, the idea that all we need to do is to listen to the "cacophony of voices to understand the democratic imperative" in the novel is simply naive (RLT, 268). Literary expression is a lot more complicated than that. What about extended verse narratives such as the Persian romantic epics, for example? Where do we place them in our perception of democratic societies? These are usually the overlapping stories of a number of significant protagonists and those around them. The stories are about love, ambition, loyalty, conflict, and more. Doesn't the love story of *Shirin and Khusrau*, by the twelfth-century poet Nizami, for instance, offer a "cacophony of voices" among its characters? Aren't the voices of Khusrau the king, his attendant Shapur, his opponent Bahram, the main female protagonist Shirin, and the master mason Farhad very different from one another? Lack of familiarity with Persian literature appears to be the main problem here. A careful look at this tale by the master storyteller of Ganjeh demonstrates that even Shabdiz and Gulrang, the horses of the two main protagonists, have different temperaments, described in detail, that make a difference to the plot.

A number of years ago, Anne, a comparative literature Ph.D. student with a great interest in Persian works, analyzed the novel *The Blind Owl* by the celebrated twentieth-century Iranian novelist and short-story writer Sadeq Hedayat. She concluded that if Bakhtin had known Persian and had read such novels, he no doubt would have modified some of his judgments. This observation contains invaluable insight. Our transnational conditions demand that theoretical analysis be carried out by experts who, in addition to command of their own tradition, know the literature produced around the globe. We can no longer afford to produce models built on the basis of a single tradition and applied randomly across cultures. Yes, the elephant has grown, but the candles are many. We no longer have to be content with a feel in the dark.

Take the celebrated Persian poet and mystic Rumi, for example. His *Masnavi* is a didactic compendium of speculative mysticism produced in rhyming couplets. You would usually expect a compendium like that to get on with its speculative analysis. Not in Rumi's case. His *Masnavi* breaks out of its generic limits and produces some of the most lyrical moments in all of classical Persian poetry. The conclusion from all of this is rather simple. Before making blanket judgments about an entire culture on the basis of a literary genre, or vice versa, it makes sense to learn about parallel and diverging generic forms within that culture — or one risks being completely off the mark. And now, to hear a voice very different from those of the protagonists you have met so far in *Women without Men*, let us get back to our novel and meet the lovely Zarrinkulah.

The fifth woman protagonist the readers meet in *Women without Men* is Zarrinkulah. Zarrinkulah, twenty-six years old, is a prostitute. That is how she is introduced to us, with no sugar coating the bitterness, no attempt to justify her standing. In other words, Parsipur is not ashamed of her, and neither should we be. She has worked in a certain brothel as long as she remembers. Once, after complaining about the pressures of working there, she was beaten, and thereafter accepted her fate. But *has* she accepted it? There is something really different about Zarrinkulah. She is not ready to be trampled by others. Her spirit is not broken. No matter what happens to her, she is full of laughter. She cracks jokes and dances for other women. That is the main reason why the women do not let her leave that brothel. The other reason is that she has no place else to go.

One day, something really strange happens to Zarrinkulah. She begins to see men without their heads. How can she speak to anyone about this? What if they think she has been possessed by a demon? What will happen to her then? She remembers another resident of the brothel who had become possessed a while ago. Her screams had driven the customers away, so she had been forced to leave. Zarrinkulah devises a solution: if she learns to sing, she will not have to scream. Every night, from that time on, she finds a quiet corner and sings to herself, despite the fact that she cannot carry a tune. One day a young woman enters the brothel and they become friends, a replacement for her out-of-tune singing. With help from this young woman, Zarrinkulah decides to pray. In order to pray, however, one first needs to perform a cleansing ritual. Zarrinkulah finds a local bath where she will be given a private space of her own. She has never been treated like a person or given a space in which to perform her own ritual.

Parsipur's skill in showing us Zarrinkulah's transformation is tremendous. There are no teachers or holy figures involved. All the purity comes from within her; from that point on, Zarrinkulah will never be violated. She will be her own person. The process of change begins in the bath itself when she breaks down and cries. By the time she leaves the public bath and heads for the local shrine, the shrine is closed. But Zarrinkulah does not need any more cleansing. The courtyard of the shrine is flooded with moonlight. She sits there bathing in the light till morning. When they open the doors of the shrine in the morning, she does not go inside. She has all the holiness she needs inside her. She is not crying anymore either. In the café where she eats porridge for breakfast, she is "a little woman of twenty-six with a heart open like the sea." No one would ever suspect that she once was a prostitute. She asks the café owner:

— Where would one go to find cool drinking water so late in the summer?
— Karaj is a good start!

By the time Zarrinkulah is on the road, we are exhausted, with both the women in the story and the reader yearning for something of a happy nature to come along. I have read this story many times and taught it in class. At this point, one usually would like to turn to Parsipur and say, "You have given me one woman who wants to become a tree, one twice-dead, one trying every trick to marry a dishonest coward, one who has killed her husband, and one whose only refuge is a brothel. What are these women doing now? They are traveling on some Godforsaken road, heading for some unknown destination. Come now, give us something good!"

Upon a closer look, however, Parsipur has given us something good.

First, she has packed her story with delightful details and told it with such frankness and humor that we have been glued to it. Secondly, she has given these women—and by extension us—a great gift: the ability to survive. Every one of our protagonists is a survivor, even the one who has died twice (or perhaps I should say, particularly the one who has died twice). The message is simple and clear. The women are saying, "We are here to stay, come oppression, murder or rape. We will suffer but won't be shattered beyond repair. We will pick up the pieces and move on." One of the hideous universal tools used to bend women into obedience has always been the power of the taboo, the disgrace attached to disasters. A woman who is raped does not just have to live with the horrors of the violation itself but with the violence done to her persona, her reputation, and her psyche. Well, not where Parsipur calls the shots.

Sure enough, there is a rape scene coming up. The journeys of women to Karaj are not described in detail except in the case of Munis and Faizeh, who are raped by a truck driver and his assistant. Even then, that is the only part of the journey we read about. It is a cold-blooded encounter made all the more horrible by the fact that the rapists treat it like a stop to get a cup of tea or smoke a cigarette. They get back into their truck afterward and even joke about the incident. Little do they know that that is the last joke of their lives. They exit the scene in an accident that kills them both, minutes after the rapes. The girls pull themselves together, hold each other's hand, and continue toward Karaj.

But the violence on the road has a purpose beyond showing the evil in the men. It transforms Karaj. Karaj is so special because getting there is not easy. Had the women been able to buy a plane ticket and reach Karaj in an hour, the destination would be nothing but a simple town outside Tehran. Now, it is the place you go to find your shattered self, to put the pieces back together and take your time deciding what you want to do. In fact, Karaj is the unfettered and brave moment you can seize to discover yourself.

There is another point Parsipur is driving home rather harshly, and, I would say, deliberately so. Discovering the world is not for sissies. It means losing the protection of home, or abandoning it because it has never *really* provided much protection. It means taking responsibility for yourself. (Well, a little magical help from Parsipur wouldn't hurt. After all this is a beginning.) Munis expresses this eloquently after they arrive, tired and injured, in Farrukhlaqa's garden:

I always wanted to see places like China and India, the world really. I wanted to understand things for myself, not to sit idle and let others explain things to me, and make a fool out of me so my life ends without comprehending anything. Of course, people say ignorance is bliss and the life of an ass is a life of happiness. But I have decided I want to know even if it means being unhappy. It's natural that when you get on the road, you face danger. Either you are strong enough to face it or you turn back and join the flock like a lamb. And sure they might shun you now like you have a disease. You can do one of two things; put up with the shunning or end your life.

It is important to realize that Karaj is not a final destination — or a place of major transformation — but a stage, or rather a station, along the way. It is a temporary shelter, but one that provides the opportunity to heal. This is the way Munis explains it with her dry humor: "Unfortunately the times are not ripe for a woman to travel alone. One has to become invisible or put up with staying home. But I am finished with staying home, and since I am supposed to be at home, I have thought of a good way to travel. I will go for a while then get myself inside a house. Then go some more and get myself inside another house. In this way, at least, I can travel in the world with the speed of a turtle."

Compromise might be necessary regarding the speed and style of moving in the world, but Parsipur is adamant about one thing. Men cannot own women, neither can they pollute them. A prostitute can be holy if she chooses to be, and a woman can leave the painful, violent experience of rape behind and be whole again. The oppressive forces of the world can hinder and hurt but cannot shatter women beyond repair. So Munis and Faizeh continue toward Karaj in spite of the assault. Should you desire a touch of irony to help reduce the bitterness of the girls' experience, there is one. The two rapists give a ride to a passenger of a completely different nature from their own. He is the "good gardener" who would serve and entertain the women. He is the only man Parsipur allows into the women's safe haven. He does not find out about the rape, survives the truck accident, and, of course, carries on with his own trip to Karaj.

The ascendance of the women begins with Farrukhlaqa's arrival in Karaj in front of the garden. We know the extent of her control by her privileged position in the back seat of the car, with the driver, the estate agent, and her housekeeper sitting up front. Parsipur tells us that all three will be discharged, even the driver, because Farrukhlaqa knows how to drive herself. She is about to see the garden. The agitated estate agent, Ustuvari, keeps praising the property: "It is a jewel Ma'am, you will see!"

Ustuvari is agitated but Farrukhlaqa is not. She takes in the beauty of the garden with thirsty eyes. A soft, joyful tremor goes through her body as she steps onto the gravel path leading to the front door of the house. The pond in front of the building is large. The structure itself is not artfully built, but it can be beautified. The front door opens into a serene and spacious hall with rooms around it. Every room has a window that opens into the garden. Farrukhlaqa thinks that the building could use a touch-up and maybe some additional rooms because there will be many guests. Ustuvari explains that the foundation is solid enough should she decide to build another floor. Then he points to a corner, indicating that if she plants a tree there, it will grow all the way to reach the second floor. Wow! A tree right inside the house? She is speechless.

As they go around the house Ustuvari tries to overcome his agitation by showing the advantages of the building. Farrukhlaqa has already developed a fantasy. She will turn this into a great house and have friends over from Tehran every Friday. Gulchehreh's bad temper and antisocial behavior had driven their friends away. "All the better," she thinks. She can start making her own friends, proper ones—writers, poets. Ustuvari now shows her the garden and looks even more troubled. "In all of Karaj, you won't find a garden this good Ma'am," he says. He exaggerates, but Farrukhlaqa does not care. She has liked the place from the first instant, she does not need his justifications. Now they are on the bank of the river. Ustuvari comments, "As you see Ma'am, this side of the garden does not have a wall. The river marks the boundary. And don't worry about burglary, the river runs really fast here. There is no danger of anyone crossing. Besides, the people around here don't engage in such things." Farrukhlaqa is not worried about burglary. She just wants to look, to listen to the sounds of the garden, to inhale it, to take it all in. And then she sees the Tree! This cannot be true. "Who is this?" she asks.

Lo and behold, there stands the source of Ustuvari's agitation, the Tree. It is a young woman. Her clothes are torn; her feet planted in the earth; her figure tall and upright, looking at them. Ustuvari has told Farrukhlaqa everything about the garden except this little detail. Now he has to answer the question, "Who is this?" Well, who *is* this? "This is, in fact, a human being but I promise you the most harmless human you have ever seen," he mumbles. Then the real story emerges. This poor woman has gone mad and planted herself in the garden. That is why the property is for sale at so reasonable a price. The family is hoping Farrukhlaqa, herself a woman, can tolerate this wretched tree. Farrukhlaqa asks why, if this woman is insane, has she not been taken to an asylum? It is complicated, Ustuvari explains. When she first disappeared her family looked for her everywhere, but they could not find her and finally stopped searching. When they came to the garden this summer they found the poor thing planted here. Ustuvari is now sobbing so hard that Farrukhlaqa thinks the woman must be a relative of his. "No Ma'am she isn't," he explains, "and I have not cried in twenty years but whenever I see her I can't stop myself." The family has tried to uproot her, but the Tree has pleaded, "Please, please don't cut me. Let me grow leaves," according to Ustuvari. "But she hasn't," observes a startled Farrukhlaqa, who has begun to like the Tree. "No, she hasn't," agrees Ustuvari. "But she has sprouted roots, maybe she will grow leaves as well next year."

Farrukhlaqa inquires about the woman's family. "Why are they so ashamed?" she asks. "Becoming a tree is not a shameful thing." Ustuvari looks puzzled. What kind of a person would become a tree? The woman's brother has not stopped crying since they found her, fearing that "there will soon be jokes about our family, calling us Treeson or Treepur." They are an old and respected family, explains Ustuvari, how can they admit they have a tree in the family? Had she become a minister or a representative in the parliament, it would have been a different story. But how does one explain a tree?

The Tree is a young woman of twenty-seven or twenty-eight. She is knee-deep in the ground. Farrukhlaqa is beginning to like her tree more and more by the minute. Ustuvari wants a confirmation: "I have told them not to worry. You are a real lady and will tolerate poor Mahdukht in your house." Farrukhlaqa is not listening. A human tree. How unique! How wonderful! No one else has ever had one. She can have her literary salon around her. Her salon will be famous in no time, and so will she. Why, she might even have an opportunity to be elected to parliament. She has always known that she has a greater capacity for accepting new things than many others. They cannot understand the value of a human tree. Well, she is not sure that she can fully understand it either, but her instinct tells her the Tree will bring good things. "We can plant the tree I was suggesting inside the house and put a wall around this one to cover the disgrace from view," Ustuvari suggests. But Farrukhlaqa ends the discussion. There is no need for a tree in the house, and this one can stay in the open. She will take her as she is.

Back in the house, there is a revolution occurring inside Farrukhlaqa. Something has been released. She not only agrees to buy the house and garden right away, she moves in. It does not matter that the house is empty. She wants to oversee the renovation herself, and wants it all done in a month. Her housekeeper, Musayyeb, reminds her that the villagers are nosy, that a quick move will reflect badly on her; she responds that she will teach them not to pester her. Suddenly there is a noise. "See!" says Musayyeb, pleased. "They are already knocking on the door." But the knockers are not nosy villagers, as you might have guessed. Parsipur has told the women that the garden is now safe and theirs to enjoy. They are arriving.

The first is Zarrinkulah accompanied by the "good gardener," whom she has encountered on the way. The gardener speaks first, in part because Zarrinkulah is a twenty-six-year-old ex-prostitute who is unsure whether she will be accepted without a reference. Furthermore, the gardener has a special purpose to fulfill. Having discovered the extraordinary tree minutes earlier, Farrukhlaqa is now about to find an extraordinary gardener. The man's face looks kind, and he claims he has a green thumb; these are more than enough credentials for Farrukhlaqa. We, might wonder, however, why this man is about to be let into the women's sanctuary. Parsipur uses an effective literary strategy to deal with our doubt. It comes as a little anecdote: "Is this your wife?" asks Farrukhlaqa, pointing to Zarrinkulah, who is standing in silence. "No Ma'am," says the gardener. "I ran into this poor woman on the road to Karaj." He describes Zarrinkulah's hysteric reaction to him, how she screamed at first, then burst into tears and threw herself down to kiss his feet. There has to be a good reason for this behavior because we do not expect Zarrinkulah to be submissive to men anymore. And there is such a reason, as explains the gardener: "she revealed that I am the first man she has seen in months who has a head attached to his body!" And thus Parsipur lets us know that the gardener can be trusted by the women.

At first, Farrukhlaqa is worried that Zarrinkulah might be crazy. The gardener explains that she once did bad things but that she has stopped. Farrukhlaqa hires them both on spot. Zarrinkulah's job interview is particularly delightful:

—Zarrinkulah, can you cook?

—No Ma'am!

—Do you know how to sweep?

—No Ma'am!

—Can you wash the dishes?

—No, I can't Ma'am!

Well, she is young, and she can learn. Besides, she knows songs and stories. Farrukhlaqa cannot wait for the house and garden to be ready. The men are sent out to bring in the rest of the furniture and arrange for the renovations to start. No sooner have the men left than there is another knock on the door. Who should it be but Munis and Faizeh at the end of their violent journey, beat up and tired. We have already heard Munis's response to Farrukhlaqa's query about their trip. She is not willing to stay safe and ignorant anymore. If learning means travel, and travel implies danger, so be it. Many people must have drowned before the first one learned to swim, she rationalizes. Faizeh, however, cannot stop crying. She is not a virgin anymore—how on earth is she going to find herself a decent husband? But she has made significant progress, insofar as she does not lie anymore. Munis can read minds anyway, a skill she soon demonstrates for Farrukhlaqa: "You wish to be elected to the parliament Ma'am, and that poor thing sitting over there was a prostitute until yesterday." Who better to live in a garden with a silent human tree than a mind reader? Munis will stay along with Faizeh, still crying over her lost virginity.

It is spring, "the garden is a real garden," and Parsipur can now afford to mend our feelings injured by watching the women endure suffering to get to Karaj. It is payback time. The residents of the garden are now free to live. It is not all leisure, for they work hard. In fact, they are renovating the house themselves. The gardener has taught them construction work, how to make mud plaster, haul the bricks, and do anything else that needs to be done. Farrukhlaqa oversees the project, driving to town from time to time, with Zarrinkulah at her side, to buy what they need. On sunny days, she sits by the pond watching the work progress. The house, with its three extra rooms, has been ready since the end of the fall. The gardener asks for permission to build himself a room in the garden on the bank of the river, facing Mahdukht the Tree. Farrukhlaqa worries that the Tree might never bloom, but the gardener promises that it will, adding "It is a human tree. It needs human milk to be properly nourished." Human milk? How is she going to get that?

As it turns out, human milk will not be that hard to find. The good gardener and Zarrinkulah are planning to marry. Faizeh contributes the idea of bringing a clergy member to perform the ceremony and make it a proper union. The gardener is adamant about performing the marriage ceremony himself, however. Munis does not object; Farrukhlaqa does not care; and the Tree needs human milk. Now Zarrinkulah's laughter fills the house. She sings, cooks, dances, and runs from place to place. She is everywhere and nowhere. Parsipur has given us a butterfly for the garden.

The women are safe and their basic needs are met. They can now think about life beyond the walls of the garden. Farrukhlaqa's goal is to enter politics and be elected to parliament. Munis has advised her to write and publish poetry, since fame is not without benefit in matters of public office. Farrukhlaqa practices hard. Guests come every Friday to enjoy her parties, the good food and drink she provides, the house's beautiful decor and trove of books. She has not revealed the existence of Mahdukht, the human tree, which the gardener says is not ready. Zarrinkulah has left the house to live with the gardener. They take care of the garden and collect dewdrops at dawn to water the Tree. The good gardener knows how to do that. The blossoming of the women is in the air. It is reflected in our hope that the Tree will bloom and Zarrinkulah will get pregnant.

The Tree begins first. One day early in the spring, it bursts into blossoms. It is a kind of multimedia blooming accompanied by singing. The whole garden is now filled with her songs. The gardener does not yet let Farrukhlaqa show the Tree to her friends. "It is not time," is all he says. Farrukhlaqa is practicing her craft of poetry and does not have much time to feel bad about not sharing her treasure with others. Munis helps with everything, though Faizeh thinks it is all absurd and meaningless (that is, when Munis is far enough away for her to think such negative thoughts without fearing that her mind will be read).

In a way, it is not Farrukhlaqa but the Tree that chooses the time to reveal itself. One day when a hundred guests are in the garden and the women, minus the pregnant Zarrinkulah, are working hard to prepare food, the Tree begins to sing. The guests forget they are hungry. It is as if drops of water are spreading themselves into flying carpets big enough for the guests to sit on and travel through the earth. It is a journey in rhythm, something of a dance, except it is so mesmerizing that arms and legs cannot move to its beats. As Farrukhlaqa enjoys the fascination of her guests traveling to the heart of the earth, Munis whispers in her ear, "Look how much sky surrounds us!" She is right. Everything is enveloped in an amazing green, even the fog is green. Rainbows appear, then their colors melt into dewdrops and drip from the edges of the leaves. At dusk, the guests leave quietly without once thinking about food.

Parsipur is not disappointed when women fail. Farrukhlaqa's poetic demands on herself are not well placed. Perhaps the same is true of her political ambitions. Her writing samples do not meet with Munis's approval, the person who knows and speaks the truth. But there are other ways to acquire fame. Perhaps employing a young painter to make portraits of her very attractive face would do the trick. Though not a poet, she has discovered the magic of her own beauty. Ironically, our young ex-prostitute is the one with greatest capacity for transformation. As the baby grows inside her and Munis and the gardener take care of her, Zarrinkulah turns more beautiful and translucent by the day. She loves to sit on the bank of the river and watch the flow of the water. After a while, she is completely transparent. Sometimes, Munis stands behind her, just because it is fun to watch the river flow through her crystal-clear body.

Faizeh does not change. She will have nothing to do with Zarrinkulah's transformation. So much fuss about a pregnancy! When she gets bored, she takes a trip to Tehran, where she accidentally passes by the house of Amir, Munis's brother. No, she is not in love with him anymore, nor does she crave married life as such. Rather, marrying him has turned into winning a contest. Amir sometimes shows up at Farrukhlaqa's parties. He comes without his little, shy, gentle, beautiful, quiet wife. "She is busy," he says, or, "She is not smart enough for these things. She is a housewife." Faizeh never misses the opportunity to announce, "I don't like housewives at all. A woman should be social. She should help her husband climb the ladder of progress. One cannot imprison oneself in the kitchen for ever." Then she asks Amir innocently, "You, for example, how long are you going to remain a simple civil servant? You must move up. The way to do that is to get to know important people. I know so many." Amir is anxious to learn if she knows Mr. Atrchian, the short, bald-headed chap with red skin. Of course she does, but she is no longer the old, simple-minded Faizeh who gives service for nothing in return.

Farrukhlaqa is reconsidering her lifestyle, too. She has had numerous portraits painted of herself and now wonders if she wants to keep the women in the garden forever. It might be best for someone with her political ambitions to set up a house in Tehran, dividing the year between Tehran and Karaj. The most important event in Munis's life happens around the same time: she discovers her need for love.

One night in midwinter, the garden suddenly fills with light. Munis, who sleeps by the window, opens her eyes and exclaims, "She is giving birth." She puts her clothes on and rushes to the end of the garden. Everything is covered with a layer of snow and completely bathed in light. It seems so clear that, at some point, all life was nothing but light. Zarrinkulah is hardly visible; the gardener is sitting by the wall mending his shoe. "We must help her," Munis says. "She will do it herself. All women do," the gardener responds. Before dawn a water lily is born. The gardener carries it carefully and places it in a pond he has prepared for this purpose. Then they go to the room where Zarrinkulah is sitting in bed with breasts full of milk. The gardener holds his wife and kisses her. Then he takes the milk to feed the Tree.

On the way back to the building, something unusual happens. Munis becomes jealous. This is as shocking to her as it is to us. She has always seemed perfect: serving others, having nothing but goodness in her heart. Now that she is jealous, she knows she has lacked something before. How could she have been perfect, if she never felt the need for love? Suddenly it is clear. The light she saw reflected love for another person. Why did she think all this time that being able to read minds was a big deal? It was really nothing but a burden. So what if she knows that Farrukhlaqa longs to be famous, that she now wants all of the women to leave her house? What can Munis do with these petty bits of knowledge? It would be great if she could, instead, predict her own ability to fall in love. Back at the house, Munis does not bother to tell Farrukhlaqa that Zarrinkulah has given birth. But no matter, for Farrukhlaqa is not really there anymore; she is already living in her future plans. "I'm leaving for Tehran today," she says. "I have rented a house there. Stay as long as you want. I'll be back next summer. Just leave the key with the gardener, if you are leaving."

Farrukhlaqa's indifference signals an important turning point: the women are now ready to leave the garden. Another birth is about to take place, that of the women. Remember, Karaj is just a stop on the way to the world. It is an important one, but nevertheless only a stop. We follow each woman for just a few more steps on their way out into the rest of the world. Mahdukht has been flourishing as a tree, surviving the winters and blooming in the spring. However, things begin to change when the gardener starts feeding her human milk. With that begins a sense of falling apart, a kind of explosion. It is not sudden, either, but like the slow journey of a pregnancy toward an inevitable birth. Of course, Mahdukht cannot remain knee-deep in earth for the rest of her life. What would become of her desire to see the world? One day she falls apart completely, becoming a big pile of seeds. A wind blows, taking her up in the air and spreading her along the surface of the river. What can she do but travel to all corners of the world?

Faizeh keeps meeting with Amir in secret. He complains about his wife; she listens. Finally, he proposes to her and she accepts. He hopes that someday Faizeh will introduce him to Atrchian, who can help him advance his career. Faizeh, for her part, hopes that Amir will someday leave his wife and live with her. She was never the traveling type anyway. Had it not been for Munis, she might never have undertaken the journey to Karaj in the first place. Munis helps the good gardener feed the tree until it explodes into seeds and travels out to the world. She hopes that the gardener will teach her the secret of falling in love, becoming light. "Not before you become darkness," he philosophizes. She knows that herself. She must experience darkness first. It is not enough to know other people's weaknesses, she must feel her own. She takes to the road again. The next thing we know, Munis is "becoming full with experience. that's all there was to it!" When she returns, she takes a bath, changes her clothes, and becomes a simple schoolteacher.

Farrukhlaqa stays in Tehran all winter. There are so many portraits painted of her that they fill a big exhibit. But the plan for entering politics is not working. She cannot return to Karaj, for what would she do with the women? She is delighted when Mr. Merrikhi, a friend of her old flame Fakhr al-Din, comes to see her. He comes again. They talk. He respects her, and one day he suggests that if they marry, Farrukhlaqa will make all the progress she wants. She accepts. He gets elected to parliament and she starts a charity. Zarrinkulah is still married to the good gardener and the lily she has given birth to is growing. One day the couple hold hands, sit on the lily, and head off, though to where we do not really know.

Women without Men, this colorful tale of self discovery, was written during the same time period highlighted in RLT, our example of the New Orientalist narrative. RLT addresses the issue of Iranian women and their access to literature. It declares, "in all great works of fiction, regardless of the grim reality they present, there is an affirmation of life against the transience of that life, an essential defiance. This affirmation lies in the way the author takes control of reality by retelling it in his own way, thus creating a new world. Every work of art, I would declare pompously, is a celebration of an act of insubordination against the betrayals, horrors and infidelities of life" (*RLT*, 47). This statement could be a description of what Parsipur achieves in *Women without Men* or any of her other novels. It is clear that in her "retelling the reality," she has "created a new world." She has celebrated and affirmed life through her act of insubordination.

But *RLT* does not mention Parsipur even in passing. It takes its own selective approach to retelling the reality of life in Iran: one in which big chunks of reality—including Parsipur's writing—disappear altogether. What does not disappear is greatly exaggerated. In this setting every girl-child Lolita's age becomes a sexual target for a man older than Humbert (*RLT*, 43). The subtext is that because the novelistic genre never developed in Iran, the tale of such horrors remains untold. Perhaps *RLT*'s goal is to tell this tale, but its exaggerations, oversights, and convenient moves between fact and fiction prevent it from achieving that aim. Instead, the book takes the rich and complicated story of postrevolutionary Iran and reduces it to the image of the blind man whose job was to censor movies and the ten-year-old who felt his dreams were "illegal" (*RLT*, 46). As for Iranian women, their life story cannot be so easily "taken from them," as the book suggests (*RLT*, 41). Not when contemporary Iran has storytellers as powerful as Shahrnush Parsipur.

Parsipur is a star brightening the way for men and women privileged to read her writings in Persian or in any language into which they have been translated. She is one of the Iranian women writers who wrote before, during, and after the Iranian Revolution of 1979 and lived in Iran until the 1990s. The silence in the New Orientalist narrative about Parsipur and others like her needs to be remedied. Hence my close reading of *Women without Men*, a simple affirmation of her towering presence in contemporary Iranian literature.

Parsipur talked to my class, which dealt with writing and rebellion, about the importance of harmony and mutual support between men and women. Some of us wished she had spoken as a strong-headed feminist. Well, she was just being herself. That is Parsipur for you. English was new to her then, and as a result the sophistication of her ideas outweighed her skill at putting them into words. "Please, please let me translate for you," I kept thinking. I so much wanted for my students to see the subtle points she was trying to make. But her decision to go it alone was Parsipur, too. She had spoken in her own words all her life and was not about to borrow a voice just because the language was new to her. So what if there were a few grammatical errors here and there?

She had brought a copy of a novel I thought was a new work for sale, called *The Simple Little Adventures of the Soul of a Tree*. It turned out to be as delightful as I had expected, only in a completely new way. It was more in line with her long realistic novels, *Dog and the Long Winter* and *Tuba and the Meaning of the Night*. I could not put the book down, thinking all the time, "How different from *Women without Men*. How many different ways of speaking she has!" Then I read in the preface that she had written the novel in the early years after the revolution. "Why didn't you publish this earlier?" I asked when I called to say how much I had enjoyed *The Simple Little Adventures*. "It is a parody of the young leftist movement in Iran," she replied. And what exactly did that have to do with not publishing it? She did not want the criticism voiced by a prominent writer to be used against an opposition that was going through a tough time already. One does not kick a person who is already down.

5

The Good, the Missing, and the Faceless
What Is Wrong with *Reading Lolita in Tehran*

We have come a long way together. I have led you from the summer nights of my childhood in Shiraz to the high school where you met my friends Zohreh and Minoo. On my way to graduate school in London, I have introduced you to the Eternal Forough, who voiced our earthly rebellion, and to my uncle the painter. You have seen the ancient silver spoon that gave me the courage to voice my discontent and caught a glimpse of the old man who had memorized an entire collection of poems. I have also shared with you many of the gifts that my family gave me, including the understanding that the sacred is immeasurable, that it has as many faces as I can uncover for myself.

In these stories, you have heard laughter and sensed generosity and love. As I went through painful experiences such as my divorce, the presence of friends, relatives, and sometimes total strangers healed me and brought color and happiness back to my life. In fact, I am touched once more by the warmth emanating from each little anecdote as I recount it to you after all these years.

I am not always sure why I must share a specific story except that I believe something in it will resonate with you. And that bit floats to the surface only after the story is told. The delight I took in the find-the-original painting game that my uncle played with us is one example. Discovering which card was the original and which the painted copy was not what really mattered in that game at all. What mattered was the joy of playing and our appreciation for his artful and dignified living.

The stories are my personal gift to you (and in some ways to me). Telling them in English, and celebrating the joyful memories they contain with you, transforms these anecdotes. You could say I remake them into little two-way bridges that keep my Iranian and American selves connected. In their new linguistic habitat, these memories will mingle and live side by side with other stories from my life for ever. And who will deny that bridge building is the thing to do in this age of transnationalism fractured by fear of terrorist acts and erroneous perceptions of each other? These are seminal moments in our history. We can overcome fear and build bridges by reaching out to those who are frequently presented as alien, or we can give in to the polarizing superficiality of rubrics such as old and new, East and West. Traditional cultures know much about fear and hope. They have had to look them in the face for centuries and search hard for solutions. They have a lot of candles in their antiquated stores, and it is time we insisted on using their light to see the elephant in its entirety.

The concepts of "old" and "traditional" are worth recovering from the pile of dubious connotations with which they have been saddled in our modern society. It would be a mistake to throw the baby out with the bath water. In our haste to modernize and globalize, we must not fall for what the social critic Anvar Majid describes as collapsing differences into a universalism that obliterates the promise of non-Western societies for enriching the world as they struggle for cultural plurality. Not every traditional difference is a hindrance. In the struggle of old and complex traditions for plurality, Majid tells us, there is hope for the emergence of alternatives born out of the coexistence of the past and the present, the new and the familiar, the continuous and the changing. In order to see the alternatives, we must first acknowledge the struggle of these cultures for plurality. The next step is even harder: we must respect them. Only then can understanding begin.

When speaking of meaningful instances in my personal experience, I add my literary/cultural analysis. This commentary is focused mostly on a harmful rhetoric infusing our modern popular culture through the lens of a New Orientalist narrative. I view this narration of the Middle East as exaggerated and oversimplified at best and fully distorted at worst. In particular, I critique the silencing nature of the narrative reflected in its selective remembering, lack of sensitivity to traditional cultures, and basic contempt for religious practice. My personal stories and analysis are meant to counter the New Orientalist narrative's tendency to amplify fear and mistrust by ignoring similarity and highlighting difference.

In this chapter, however, I will shift the gaze from my personal stories and focus closely on the work that I have used throughout *Jasmine and Stars* as a typical example of the New Orientalist narrative, namely *Reading Lolita in Tehran* (RLT). It is vital to provide a condensed and concrete critique of the aspects of this work that foster otherness and difference. In our close reading, RLT's perspective on contemporary Iran is shown to be one-sided and extreme, in fact as extreme as the views of the revolutionaries it criticizes. Similarly, the book's erasure of the voices of sanity reduces the entire culture to the behavior of its extremists. Before I start the critique, however, let me give you a summary of RLT. In particular, it will help for you to see the names of the seven young women in the reading group and those of the major villains, as I shall refer to them repeatedly it this chapter.

A Brief Plot Summary

RLT does not follow a continuous and unfolding plot. The best way to understand the structure of its content is to take a look at its various sections.

Essentially, the book is the author's exchanges with her seven female students embedded in anecdotes that occur in weekly reading sessions. The young women are Manna, Mahshid, Nassrin, Yassi, Azin, Mitra, and Sanaz, all in their late teens or early twenties. While the group meets between 1995 and 1997, the author's recollection of her life experience in Iran stretches from 1979 to 1997. The main writers read and discussed in the group are Vladimir Nabokov, F. Scott Fitzgerald, Henry James, and Jane Austen. The book devotes a part to each one of them.

Part I attends to Nabokov's *Invitation to a Beheading* first, drawing a parallel between its chilling atmosphere and the environment created by the Islamic Republic. The main focus of this part, however, is *Lolita*, with the seduced girl child presented to us as a metaphor for Iranian society violated by the revolutionary forces. Part II contains discussions of Fitzgerald's *The Great Gatsby* while at the same time touching on social events such as the purging of certain "antirevolutionary" faculty from the universities and the taking of the American hostages.

Part III opens with reference to the Iran-Iraq war beginning in 1980. Its literary focus is on James, his personality, and his lobbying Americans to enter World War II in support of Britain. Thereafter, we read about the women characters in *Washington Square* and *Daisy Miller*. Like the rest of the book, this part makes many allusions to the misfortunes of the local population, including a female leftist student named Razieh who is executed and an unnamed male student who burns himself to death. Part IV, which follows a format similar to that of the preceding part, is centered on female characters from Austen's novels and their rebellion against conventions. This last part winds down with Nafisi's personal thoughts about leaving Iran. Finally, a brief epilogue brings us up to date with the author's current life in the United States. It also touches on the fate of the group since the author's departure and alludes to much that has changed in "appearance" since then (341*).

Throughout, the book is peppered with references to Muslim males and/or villains. These are colleagues or students whom we do not get to know but whose behaviors represent the extremist ideals of the revolution. Unlike the female students, we do not learn their first names. Prominent among these are Messrs. Forsati, Ghomi, Bahri, Nyazi, and Nahvi.

Like the revolutionaries it criticizes, RLT speaks from a vantage point of moral goodness and superiority. The degree of heroism implied by the author's act of teaching Western fiction writers is astonishing. The students' smiles are described as "meant to tell" how crucial it was for the teaching to continue "at all costs to myself or them" (68). The uninformed reader is hence encouraged to assume that reading Western literature is forbidden in postrevolutionary Iran, an act so risky it could endanger the reader's life.

The extremists' perception of the universe as a black-and-white world of infidelity and faith is replicated by RLT's oversimplified world that posits good on the side of the West and evil squarely in the Muslim camp. The book's villains are often reduced to the basic essence of their primitive otherness: a blind adherence to their faith, hatred for progress (exemplified by the West), and the oppression of women. This last is portrayed as a repressed, savage "sexual frenzy" surfacing at public events such as mourning for dead leaders. In effect, the reader finds a harem filled with beatings, floggings, even an occasional dance behind closed doors (90, 244, 265). In the currently fragmented relations between East and West, such exaggerated and simplistic portrayals are dangerous.

By and large, RLT satisfies mass curiosity and affirms preexisting perceptions. Its central message to the reader, delivered by a member of the native culture, is: Meet the subhumans you always knew were there! Comparing the extremist student Nahvi to Elizabeth Bennet, RLT declares, "you are as different as man and mouse" (290). This assertion reflects the book's central thesis that Iranian Muslim revolutionaries are subhuman. They cannot understand any language other than brute force and do not deserve anything but our "eternal contempt" (288).

*All parenthetical page citations in this chapter refer to *Reading Lolita in Tehran*.

Flying airplanes into buildings, keeping prisoners of war out of reach of the law, beheading those who might vaguely sympathize with the "enemy," setting off bombs in subway cars, and dragging the largest army of the world halfway across the globe to fight imaginary weapons of mass destruction are signs of big trouble. This environment festering with suspicion and hatred needs a more sophisticated global perspective, one geared toward respect, recognition, and healing.

Let us now turn to specific examples of what I consider serious flaws in RLT.

Typological Problems

Examples of particular character types represented in RLT exhibit little complexity or nuance and share few traits with those of other types. They form simple, clear categories with perfectly predictable behavior. The actions of individuals are colored by and interpreted through these expectations. The type I call the Ugly are a good example. Take Nahvi, the activist Muslim student. He is committed to the values propagated by the Islamic revolution and is expected to behave accordingly. He causes a lot of discomfort by declaring his preference for the revolutionary protagonist of Gorky's *Mother* over Austen's young ladies, a proclamation not unexpected of an undergraduate living in the immediate aftermath of a revolution. He is considered less than human for expressing the opinion and is dismissed with author's "eternal contempt" (288–90). This incident is characteristic of the typological perspective that RLT offers the reader: simple and full of sharp contrasts between good and evil. The book is infested with masses of the Ugly, often called simply "they," disappearing in dark corners and resurfacing again. Like the Borg in the fictional world of Star Trek, they all have the same thoughts. They are absolutist monsters who have no individuality and do not generally disagree with each other (if they do, it means their commitment to religion is insincere). They do not change, and they most definitely do not grow. The division between them and the rest of the world is viewed as permanent. Those who belong to the Ugly but display unpredictable behavior such as reading books by Western thinkers or wearing blue jeans and Reeboks are therefore perceived as crossing the border and betraying their political and religious beliefs (280). They are viewed as hypocritical. The category of ugly has its subdivisions.

The Ugly: Variations on a Theme

The Ugly have ugly names, too, often not innocuous ones. Nahvi's name means "Arabic grammarian." His dislike for Austen's ladies is minor compared to that of some students who are presented as ready to kill the fictional figures. Ruhi ("spiritual") wears her chador in a menacing way. Ghomi ("from the city of Ghom," where major religious seminaries are located) thinks Daisy Miller is evil and deserves to die (195). Forsati ("opportunist") is an activist colleague with a character fluke, a passion for cinema. You might think that a redeeming quality, an indication that "they" are not all monsters. He is a fan of Tom Hanks, which means he is interested in American cinema and culture. For Mr. Opportunist, head of the Islamic Jihad, however, this interest means hypocrisy. The truth, RLT explains, is that Forsati is a Muslim "not particularly devoted to the religious ideals." His interest "first and foremost is in getting ahead" (206, 193). Forsati is later described as "not very creative himself . . . his creativity goes into a benign sense of self-promotion" (239). We have no proof of this self-promoting quality except that he brings American films for RLT's author and helps organize cultural events. Mr. Opportunist's lack of creativity is typical of the Ugly. Whether their goals are absolutist and self-serving or not, "they" are unable to attain them. They are — without exception — deprived of any talent. Another member of the type, a coworker of the author by the name Mrs. Rezvan ("paradise"), has literary ambitions, but she too has "limited" talents (293).

"They" are not just cruel or opportunistic. They basically have no principles. They all lie, even those who come to mourn Ayatollah Khomeini's death, since alongside the frenzy of beating chests and fainting they sit on the roadside to eat their sandwiches and drink their soft drinks as if they were on some kind of holiday or picnic. Similarly, when Iraq attacks and the war starts, the Ugly extort "undeserved privileges from the faculty" in the name of war efforts. They are ignorant, too. Even their translators and critics confuse Henry James for James Joyce. In their ignorance, they wish to kill writers as well as fictional characters (244, 193, 201).

The Ugly are cowards, too. The revolutionary guards arriving to face an armed militia in the author's house hide behind the woman servant of the house. These guards approach bombed sites after air raids "timidly." And they all hate decent people. The relatively more acceptable revolutionary student Razieh — more acceptable because she is later executed — is full of anger and hatred. "We envy people like you and want to be you," she says one day, "but we can't, so we destroy you." It is not clear whether this "you" refers to the professors, upper classes, the West, or all combined. She just hates and wishes to destroy. Whatever she means, after going through *RLT*'s filter, her words affirm the theory advanced by the more comfortable classes who see no point in analyzing the thought of activists because they are expected to boil down to envy and hatred. For a "revolutionary" who dies to preserve her ideal, Razieh has a pretty poor opinion of herself and of the masses (222).

Lack of confidence and self-respect is typical of the majority of Iranians portrayed in *RLT*. The female students are often portrayed as feeling envious of the courage displayed by Western fictional figures such as Daisy Miller. They have a confused image of themselves. The institutions are even worse. The university does not organize talks or films. The bleakness of the human landscape is such that if you have not been to Iran, it is hard to avoid pity and disdain for its people. Even if you are familiar with Iran, these feelings are hard to avoid (200, 189, 38).

Little by little, you begin to see that the contempt expressed in *RLT* has deeper and more complicated roots that positive events do not change. A revealing instance is the passage about the showing in Tehran in the 1980s of a movie made by the Russian filmmaker Andrei Tarkovsky. A large crowd has turned up at the theater to see the film. Tarkovsky is generally not known to average moviegoers anywhere. That a good crowd has come should be a positive sign. In a European city such a turnout would likely be seen as an indication of cultured behavior. *RLT*, however, does not extend such a positive judgment to the Iranian crowd. Instead, it expresses surprise at the interest of the audience, "most of whom would not have known how to spell Tarkovsky's name." How is this fact determined? We do not find out (206).

Women

Although the Ugly are all backward, subhuman, and ready to surrender to authority, women in *RLT* are particularly so. It is true that a traditionalist wave in Iran has promoted (and continues to promote) the cult of domesticity and motherhood in the aftermath of the revolution. Legal reform in areas related to gender is needed, as is also the case regarding the rights of religious minorities and election laws. But the traditional articulations of women's role are not unanimously endorsed, not even among Islamist movements. Secondly, this perception does not correspond to the reality of women's public participation in postrevolutionary Iran. Women are everywhere, including in the legislative body. Iranian men and women have engaged in reform-oriented activism since the revolution. Shirin Ebadi, the recipient of the 2003 Nobel Peace Prize, is one such activist.

In RLT, this awareness or activism is not detectable. We are instead reminded of the misery and oppression of women. The young and self-demeaning revolutionary Razieh tells her teacher, "you must think about where we are coming from. Most of these girls [her female classmates] have never had anyone praise them for anything. They have never been told that they are any good or that they should think independently. Now you come in and confront them" (221). The book reinforces this narration of Iranian women through repetition of negative and erasure of positive experiences. An American reader will likely take this as the full picture. Even an Iranian American who undertakes brief, infrequent visits to Iran may begin to doubt positive memories. The enigmatic question is, "How could the book show no awareness of the presence of intelligent, vibrant, and complicated women in that society?"

An array of exaggerated, tragic events befalls the women featured in RLT. These tragedies are described down to the finest, most excruciating detail. Revolutions are never short of tragedies. If the account of the twelve-year-old girl shot to death as she ran around the prison asking for her mother is true, it will not be the first time that ideological conviction overcame humanity (191). Neither would anyone, even the most hard-line among the revolutionaries, wear that crime as a badge of honor.

However, RLT never leaves the ominous shadow of these incidents. The women are simply doomed. When facts are not clear, it imagines the catastrophic details. Perhaps Razieh, who loved the work of James, faced the firing squad on the night the author was reading *The Long Goodbye* or *The Bostonians*. Speculations are equally grim. We are told that Mahtab, Razieh's friend who escaped execution and was released from jail, is worse off than her dead friend. Why? No explanation is provided. Similarly, when the engagement of Sanaz, one of the girls in the reading group, is broken, the incident is given the dimensions of a national disaster. In RLT, even nail polish can be described in a sorrowful tone: "It makes me happy, she [group member Azin] said, in a thin voice that did not suggest any trace of happiness. It is so red it takes my mind off things" (219, 278–79, 271).

The reader, therefore, moves from disaster to disaster without a moment's relief: compulsory wearing of the veil, seclusion, divorce, physical violence, genital mutilation! The reference to this latter is revealing. Technically, RLT should not include this particular crime because it has never been practiced in Iran. But Nassrin has been "reading Nawal al-Sadawi's book on brutality against women in some Muslim societies." So we hear about this brand of oppression by Muslims all the same (70).

More disturbing than RLT's coverage of these unending tragedies befalling the women is the suggestion that the women subjected to these cruelties have accepted, agreed with, even—deep down—enjoyed the punishments inflicted upon them. Sanaz has been subjected to flogging for no reason. We are then told: "In some perverse way, the physical punishment was a source of satisfaction to her. A compensation for having yielded to those other humiliations" (73). The women, in other words, are turned masochistic by the punishment. RLT has another category of people as disdained and misrepresented as women: the Faceless.

The Faceless

The Faceless comprise a subcategory of the ugly Muslim men. In a sense, they are the most unfairly treated because they do not have a voice. We do not know their names, nor do we hear them quoted, even indirectly. They are male and are somehow related to one of the girls we have met in the group. We know that these men are cruel and heartless to their female relatives, which has something to do with their religious convictions. Sanaz's brother is one such man. He has made it his business to make her life miserable by interfering in everything she does. Nassrin's father is another. His relatives wear the chador, and his daughter has to lie to him about going to the reading group—she tells him she is working on a translation project. Mahshid and Azin are also in contact with abusive males who fall in the category of the Faceless. Mahshid's boss bothers her at work, and Azin's husband abuses her at home. That is all we know about these two men.

Physical and psychological abuse of women is pervasive around the world. Iran is no exception. Reforms such as establishing shelters for abused women and providing women with better work opportunities and greater economic independence are needed. RLT's concern over the physical and psychological abuse of women is justified. However, it blames Iranian men for events that happen everywhere and are considered ordinary. For instance, Sanaz's fiancé, who lives in Europe, has doubts about his own readiness for marriage. He calls apologetically and breaks the engagement, "pleading" that "he would always love her." The author's comment about the young man is short and clear: "bloody coward" (278).

Even men who do not break engagements are not any better. Yassi tells the members of the reading group that she has had a suitor. As they walk in the park to get acquainted, she teases him by starting to walk fast all of a sudden. "The idiot" does not even ask her why she is suddenly walking faster. He just tries "out of politeness" to fall into step with her (284). Yassi has a right not to wish to marry a traditional suitor, but politeness is not a justified source for disdain. Nassrin, Azin, and Sanaz use the same tone when they talk about their respective father, husband, and brother. They tell us that these men physically "abuse," "dictate" their will, "forbid" learning, and "confiscate" the women's possessions, among other things (48, 54, 17, 15). Since we do not hear the men's voices, or see them in any other context in the book, they remain a faceless, menacing force throughout.

The Ugliest

The Faceless are members in the category of the Ugliest, which requires one major qualification: believing in Islam. It is not necessary to list all the examples of this type, for they are the majority of the Muslim men and women featured in RLT. Although unflattering literature on Islam is not hard to find these days, it is difficult to find a fuller Islamization of wickedness than the one configured by RLT, particularly among works that are not expressly a commentary on Islam.

The book's anger is not directed at traditional culture in general but is specifically targeted at Islam. The handful of non-Muslim Iranian men who are introduced, although brought up in the same larger culture, are immune to the ills that the lives of Muslims demonstrate. The "kid" is an honest, brilliant, loving, and courageous Baha'i boy whom we read about because of the death of his grandmother. He does not know what to do because "there were no burial places for Baha'is" (230). This information is contradicted later by the assertion that opponents of the regime and Baha'is were denied headstones and were thrown into common graves (244). Still, neither situation is desirable. Baha'is did suffer persecution due to their religious beliefs, particularly in the early years after the revolution.

The issue here is the black-and-white contrast presented between the brilliance and honesty of the Baha'i boy caught in the horrors of Muslim hypocrisy and the weak personality of the Muslims he deals with. The "kid" has fallen in love with a "Muslim girl." She marries a "rich older man" for opportunistic reasons but apparently hangs on to her affections for the "kid," later trying "to make up with him as a married woman" (229). Here, religion is the primary determinant of moral behavior and gender is irrelevant. RLT provides many examples of corrupt Muslim behavior. Most of these incidents are followed by commentary on the absolutist and fanatical nature of Islam.

The Mythical Monster: Islam

The Islamization of wickedness is one side of the conceptual coin. The other side is the book's efforts to reward American readers with the unqualified association of good things with the West. I call this the Westernization of goodness. It is related to a larger problem, the sharp contrast depicted between good and evil in RLT's fairy tale environment. Here, the main intention is to support the good forces of an imaginary West in its fight against the horrors of an imaginary Islam. The problem is deeper than exaggeration and uninformed anger; rather it is the creation of a mythical monster presented to us as Islam.

This is not a conflict between belief and disbelief. Each one of us is free to follow any religion or none at all. The issue at stake is the way the nature and functions of religion are conceptualized and understood. Let me give you an example through RLT's comment on a male Muslim student, Bahri. Here Bahri's simultaneously timid and arrogant personality is explained: "I grew more accustomed to his special kind of arrogance, that of a naturally shy and reserved young man who had discovered an absolutist refuge called Islam" (103). Absolutism is here located within Bahri's religion itself rather than in the way he practices his beliefs. Essentialization of any belief system is fundamentally naive. It views the religion as a tailored dress that one puts on rather than a living practice that is colored by personal choices and social conditions. According to this assumption, a Muslim wears an "absolutist" straitjacket no matter how thoughtful, reasonable, or analytical she or he may be. Conversely, a person with secularist tendencies (even my geneticist friend who will not question or reexamine his understanding of religion) can not be an absolutist. This essentialization colors all RLT's statements about Islam.

Elsewhere, the book refers to the "myth of Islamic feminism," which is qualified as a "contradiction in terms" (262). This perspective is hampered by two problems. The first is conceptualizing religion as the straitjacket that prevents an individual from desiring change of the kind feminists wish to see. This implies that not only believing Muslims but Christians, Jews, and other religious people would likewise be unable to desire improvement in women's rights and conditions. The second problem is that studies of life in postrevolutionary Iran do not justify excluding the lively gender debates that have taken place in the country among men and women of all backgrounds. These debates have kept women's rights issues on the agenda of the policy makers. Not all goals related to the rights of women have been achieved. But to deny that modern Iranian Muslims are pursuing this lively debate is astonishing. According to *RLT*, the myth of Islamic feminism was perpetuated by the authorities because it "enabled the rulers to have their cake and eat it too: they could claim to be progressive and Islamic" at the same time (262).

RLT displays ignorance about religious aspects of life in Iran. Vague and general explanations result: "to say that he was *active* [in the Muslim Student Association] meant that he was one of the more fanatical" (250). Matters related to Islamic law are particularly inaccurate. Azin says, "this guy [President Khatami] wants the rule of law? Isn't this the same law that allows my husband to beat me and take my daughter away?" (318). The answer is no. Currently, physical abuse affords legal ground for divorce in Iran; and child custody is not automatically given to either parent (except in the case of girls, who remain with their mothers until the age of seven, when the court rules on custody). Unsympathetic judges, abusive husbands, and women unaware of their legal rights can indeed be found in Iran. But they are neither an Iranian nor a Muslim novelty.

I have divorced friends in the United States who cannot leave the state in which they live without informing the court of their move, whereas their ex-husbands — even if they were the ones who walked out of the marriage and away from the child — do not have that obligation. Worse still is the case of a friend who lived for years after her divorce in the horror of harm coming to her young daughter. Her ex-husband had a history of institutionalization and abusive behavior; he took the child away periodically and threatened to harm her. The mother never succeeded in persuading the judge — who refused to limit the father's visitation rights — of the nightmare she lived in. Her Catholic family had objected to the divorce and was not sympathetic to helping her. Conditions improved only after her daughter grew old enough to protect herself.

In some cases, RLT's perspective concerning religious laws is so distorted as to be almost funny. Laws of ritual purity are among those that are hopelessly misinterpreted. The book explains that "good Muslims" consider all non-Muslims dirty and do not eat from the same dishes (180). In fact, Muslim dietary laws are less elaborate than their counterparts in some other religions such as the Jewish faith. Furthermore, as in Judaism, these rules are not about dirtiness; they are about observing a ritual. In Iran, too, there are extreme and relaxed approaches to dietary law as well as to other issues. I regularly ate in my Armenian friends' homes and brought food and sweets back and forth. RLT promotes the view that Muslims are all one and the same. What is more, their lives consist of nothing other than their religion. This reductionism is echoed in the words of reading group member Yassi: "Our religion has defined every single action we have taken. If one day I lose my faith, it will be like dying and having to start new again in a world without guarantees" (327). Through RLT's Islamophobic lens, religion does not enrich a life; it totally takes it over.

The book's discussion of Islam cannot be closed without a word about the Islamic Republic. The Islamic regime, which came to power with the 1979 revolution, was a political governing force driven by the totalizing vision of the revolution, focused on establishing its hegemony over a diverse society. Like its counterparts elsewhere, it espoused a purist outlook, suffered from internal conflict, and used far too much force to assert its authority. These practices led to undesirable social conditions for the average citizen.

RLT, however, presents the Islamic regime as a monster lurking in the background with "thoughts," "tasks," "intentions," and "actions" that portray the regime as a single being possessing a unified will. For example, arguing against the belief that "the personal is political," the book reminds the reader: "the realm of imagination is a bridge between them [personal and political], constantly refashioning one in terms of the other." The Islamic Republic "knows" this, and "not surprisingly" its "first task" has been to blur the lines and boundaries between the personal and the political, thereby destroying both. Thus, the regime is endowed with a homogeneous and unified body of thought and action (273).

The Islamic Republic prowls in the dark, conspiring to fool people to come out of hiding so that it may destroy them. There is no indication that this regime is, like any other, made of a group of people themselves subject to change, with view points that converge on certain issues and diverge on others. Since the regime is not perceived to be made up of individual persons, the conflicts its members have with each other, the extreme acts that some commit with which others disagree, the wrongdoings and bitter disillusionments, are not portrayed as the struggles of a society going through a painful learning experience. These are instead diseases of the deranged mythical monster that is Islam.

When the Iran-Iraq war ended in 1988, finally a little room was opened for the larger public to put the idea of reform on the agenda. The less flexible elements within the regime resisted such an opening up, while the more open-minded rejoiced. In *RLT*, this development is not portrayed in these terms. Such pluralistic tendencies and differences of opinion are expected of "normal" societies, but not those tainted by Islamic beliefs. Differences of opinion are instead an indication that those in the regime are "disillusioned" with Islam. "Confronted with the ideological void," they attack each other out of frustration. In such degenerated societies, *RLT* tells the reader, peace only makes things worse. It leads to the release of "evil spirits trapped in the bottle" (274). There is no suggestion that what we might be seeing is a society trying to move forward, one experimenting with democratization and making utterly painful mistakes. Instead, it is a conspiracy, a fairy tale gone wrong, "in which all the good fairies had gone on strike, leaving us stranded in the middle of a forest not far from the wicked witch's candy house" (241).

If evil Muslim behavior is one side of the societal coin, the other side of the coin in *RLT* is the unconditional goodness of things Western. The West has minor disadvantages and weaknesses. Daisy Miller, for example, cannot perform a dance as seductive as that of the student Sanaz. But this deficiency aside, the West possesses all that is beautiful and good. The ability to do things such as speak one's mind, make a film, write a story, or publish a book are presented as inherently Western qualities. In 1994, the Ministry of Islamic Culture and Guidance publishes a book by *RLT*'s author on Nabokov, and the Farabi Film Foundation shows works of progressive directors. *RLT* notes these actions on the Iranian cultural front, actions that might be viewed as indications of a move forward, of genuine social change. But the "truth," according to the book, is that "having nowhere to turn to," the Muslims are returning to the "Western democracies they had once so vehemently opposed." They may not admit it, but their desire to be like the West betrays their true feeling (277, 276).

The above observation is coupled with another about the reasons why the bad guys are disturbed by Jane Austen: "Just as they censored colors and tones of reality to suit their black-and-white world, they censored any form of interiority in fiction" (277). In reality, more than one black-and-white world is on view here, and the one promoted by RLT is no less extreme than the one it opposes. A clarification is in order, too: I am not aware that any of Austen's novels have been censored in Iran either before or after the revolution. *Pride and Prejudice* remains a very popular novel there to this day.

The Missing

Entire groups of Iranians who lived and produced significant work before, during, and after the revolution are totally erased from the image of Iran in RLT. Many are neither particularly religious/revolutionary, antirevolutionary, nor for or against the West. Most love their country, respect other people's beliefs, do not support extremism or war, and love to see a democratic system that respects their culture and tradition continue to develop in Iran. They complain about the unequal distribution of power in the world. When the law of the land prevents certain candidates from competing in the Iranian elections, reformists are jailed, and newspapers are closed, these people feel deeply hurt. When the U.S. Army invades Iraq in the name of democracy, they feel hurt, too. They will not be co-opted, bribed, labeled, intimidated, accused, or made to disappear. They go about living a quiet, humane, honorable life; no one gets to hear about them because they do not write slogans on the wall or attach bombs to themselves.

The sad fact is that members of this category are often not deemed newsworthy. Except in rare instances, the world does not get to know them or their fabulous creations. Fortunately, their creative work is cherished deeply by others who live in present-day Iran. Since their group is large, I limit myself to the subjects of literature, cinema, philosophy/social criticism, and law. I call this category the Missing because, like the jasmine and stars of my life, these wondrous people are absent from New Orientalist works such as RLT.

The Missing have created, published, and staged much of their works in the period since the revolution. Furthermore, the degree of influence they exert on contemporary Iranian culture is incomparably larger than that of the villains introduced in RLT. I can only guess that they are left out of the picture because if they were included the perfect darkness portrayed by the book would be diluted. Whatever the reason, they are missing all the same. Despite the limited number of the subjects that I have selected, I can only describe a small number of the major figures in each subject. Discussing them at length is out of the question here.

I will start with poets, mentioning only two. First, there is the Lady of contemporary Persian Ghazal writing, one of the best poets of this century, Simin Behbahani. Behbahani, whom Iranians affectionately call Simin, is also known as the Lioness of Iran. Having published numerous collections of poems, she is one of the most prominent public figures in the country. She has spoken out against war, violence, and oppression of every kind. Her personal temperament is that of a secular intellectual, but her work is neither antagonistic nor insensitive to religion. *A Line of Speed and Fire*, *Paper Dress*, and *A Windowful of Freedom* are among her latest collections. Iranian critics study the depth of her poetic art. Many doctoral students write their dissertations on her work, and Iranian media features her on a regular basis. She continues to live and work in Iran.

The second figure is Mohammad Reza Shafi'i-Kadkani, an expressly Muslim poet. You would be hard pressed to find anyone more outspoken against tyranny. Shafi'i-Kadkani has published a vast quantity of generically varied poetry as well as literary criticism, as an academic, in the field of comparative literature. Graduate students from all over the country correspond with him, come to listen to his talks, or consult with him about the topic of their research. *In Nishabour Garden Alleys*, *From Naught to Singing*, and *Like Trees in a Rainy Night* are among his better-known works. I make a point of visiting him at his house each time I return to Iran. Three conditions are present in every visit. The first is that the phone is ringing off the hook with would-be visitors hoping to get a half-hour with him. The second is that he usually has a new book that he graciously gifts to me. The third is that I know I am walking out of his house with a soon-to-be classic in the study of Persian literature.

In the area of philosophy and social criticism, Abdulkarim Soroush is well known to the world, one of a panorama of figures ranging from secular to deeply religious publishing in Persian on the subject. Soroush stands out of the crowd for his intellectual versatility. Steeped in traditional religious learning and equally well trained in Western thought and philosophy, he is best known for his iconoclastic attempts to reinvigorate religious thought in postrevolutionary Iran. His *Contraction and Expansion of the Shari'a* is among the most controversial compositions. Despite the sophistication of his approach, his critical writings sell thousands of copies in a matter of weeks. Last year when I visited a bookstore in Iran, the young Shirazi bookseller knew every single title by Soroush plus the contents of the works. I was looking for one of his earlier commentaries on the subject of time as movement in the essence of entities written by a seventeenth-century philosopher known as Sadra al-Din Shirazi. For some reason I had blanked out on the title. It took a slight reference to the subject for the bookseller to walk right to the shelf and walk back with the text.

In the area of law and human rights, Nobel laureate Shirin Ebadi is a person to remember. A lawyer by profession, Ebadi was known to Iranians for her efforts to improve the rights of women and children long before she received her Nobel Prize. She rose to further prominence due to her willingness to serve in a series of extremely sensitive, high-profile cases of political crime that involved the assassination of Iranian intellectuals. In accepting some of these cases Ebadi took considerable risk, because they implicated certain government officials. At the same time, she lavished equal attention on a murder case involving a young girl of modest background. Ebadi continues to live, speak, and write in Iran, and has published on her favorite subject of legal reform.

Despite *RLT*'s repeated references to the "blind censor," Iranian cinema is alive and well. In fact, it experienced its most flourishing period after the revolution. Abbas Kiarostami is by far the best known among contemporary Iranian filmmakers, known to most for *Taste of Cherry*, which earned him the Cannes Film Festival Award. Kiarostami has made many films in his realistic style, managing consistently to stay above an artificial "Islam versus the West" dichotomy. He rose to prominence in the West with his 1978 film *Where Is the Friend's House*, inspired by a poem with the same title by the renowned contemporary Iranian poet Sohrab Sepehri. Kiarostami lives in Iran and takes his camera to the remotest of villages. His 2000 film *The Wind Will Take Us* was also inspired by — and named after — a poem, this time one by the Eternal Forough. It takes place in a Kurdish village.

Postrevolutionary Iranian cinema has many more stars, among them women with distinct voices. Tahmineh Milani has become the most ardent critic of misogyny. Ahmet, I, the children, and a few cousins saw her *Two Women* at a movie theater in Shiraz in 1999. It is an epic tale of a young woman's courage and resistance in the face of gender inequality. My cousin

Mahyar had to go early and stand in line for an hour to buy us tickets. A theater full of people cheered as the movie ended with the woman emerging from tragic events and thinking out loud about resuming her long-abandoned university education. Another major woman writer and director in current Iranian cinema is Rakhshan Bani Itemad. In most of her works, she combines in-depth social criticism with lyrical story telling. Her *Under the Skin of the City* celebrates the strength and charisma of a woman factory worker. Neither Bani Itemad nor Milani display strong religious tendencies. Their male counterpart, Mohsen Makhmalbaf, does. In fact, Makhmalbaf offers a classic example of an Iranian artist with deep-seated Muslim convictions who, at the same time, remains an outspoken critic of the Islamic Republic. Makhmalbaf, his wife Marzieh, and their children Samira, Maysam, and Hana, have each made delightful and critically acclaimed movies. To see the achievements of this amazing family, visit *Makhmalbaf Film House* on the Web. The Makhmalbafs continue to live and work in Iran, as do many more trend-setting filmmakers such as Beiza'i and Mehrjooi, whom we will not be able to fit in here.

As I was about to close this section devoted to the Missing, a rather strange coincidence happened. I received a note from my ex-student Anne, who has a special eye for cultural matters as well as a great memory. She never neglects to bring to my attention important details such as this one that might have slipped past me. She had sent a clipping from the *New York Times*, dated July 13, 2005, about Karim Emami, the celebrated Iranian translator who rendered *The Great Gatsby* and John Osborne's *Look Back in Anger* into Persian. Emami had died at age 75 at his home in Tehran. I look at the note and think, "Of course, those! The great translators of Western literature into Persian!" I have not even mentioned them. People in all cultures translate, but there may be no exact parallel in American culture for the role that Emami and his counterparts play in Iran. Let me explain.

Iranian readers are so interested in world literature that good translators can become almost as famous as authors themselves. Najaf Daryabandari, Mohammad Ghazi, Hasan Shahbaz, Simin Danishvar, and Jalal AleAhmad (the last two prominent writers themselves) are only a few of the better-known names. James, Austen, Fitzgerald, Maupassant, Steinbeck, Camus, Faulkner, Brecht, and many others became familiar names among Iranian readers long before RLT was written. I end my brief account of the Missing by telling you a little more about Karim Emami, who was born in 1930 into a Tehrani merchant family. Having studied English literature at Tehran

University, Karim and his wife Goli, also a translator, started a bookstore called Zamineh that became a meeting place for book lovers. In addition to providing translations, he worked as a journalist. Karim Emami was taken from us by leukemia, the disease that also claimed Edward Said, one of the greatest minds in twentieth-century social and literary criticism and the first to pay critical attention to the phenomenon of Orientalism.

In describing a few of the Missing, I have left out entire subjects, each boasting their own bright stars. Painting, theater, novels and short stories, journalism, and sports are among these. There is simply not enough room to do them all justice. As a work mourning the absence of cultural/artistic complexity in postrevolutionary Iran, RLT could have paid attention to some of these important and celebrated figures. Had this happened, the reader would have viewed a totally different picture. The cultural landscape portrayed in the book would not have turned frightening, bleak, and barren. Ironically, the handful of intellectuals mentioned by the book with reference to their contributions are victims. These are the individuals who lost their lives or went missing during the wave of terror and assassination against Iranian intellectuals in the 1990s (308–10).

There is no justification for the erasure of all these figures. I can only guess that they are erased because their presence would have disproved the theory suggesting a complete Iranian collapse in the absence of the West. Their voices would have contradicted RLT's perspective in other ways, too. Many of the figures mentioned here speak up against oppression in an effort to improve human and civil rights in Iran, but they remain equally critical of the West. In other words, they stand neither on the side of the Ugly in the memoir nor on the side of the Good. Hence RLT does what undemocratic regimes do to their vocal opponents: It makes them disappear.

The Good

Let us now turn to another character type identifiable in RLT: the Good. In the book's fairy tale universe, there is no doubt as to the identity of the good fairies. They are all American. RLT's account details the horrors of a revolution opposing America and its foreign policy, yet there is not a single statement implying that America is responsible for the slightest direct or indirect involvement. All criticism of America is presented to us as misinformed, ill-intentioned, misplaced, and exaggerated. This is a major betrayal of the American reader, one typical of the New Orientalist narrative.

Let me explain by way of a metaphor borrowed from Nabokov's critique of totalitarianism. In the novel *Invitation to a Beheading*, which RLT showcases, the jailer invites the jailed protagonist Cincinnatus to a dance. Cincinnatus enjoys the attention from the jailer so much that he regrets the ending of the "friendly embrace" when the dance ends. The interpretation given for this is that "as long as he accepts the sham world the jailers impose upon him, Cincinnatus will remain their prisoner and will move within the circles of their creation" (76). Ironically, RLT has created a world parallel to that of Cincinnatus's jailer for the American reader. To get an independent, balanced, and fair perspective on the subjects discussed in the book, the reader needs to stop dancing with the jailer and break out of RLT's exaggerated world. Let us consider a few specific examples of the way this created world is sustained and presented to the good fairy, the American.

From the opening pages, Western readers are advised that they are fundamentally different from backward-looking Iranians whose culture is not interested in the future. "I told them [her students] . . . we in ancient countries have our past—we obsess over the past. They, the Americans, have a dream: they feel nostalgic about the promise of the future." Before the reader can question the validity of her sweeping characterizations of two entire cultures (one looking forward and one looking back), the memoir bolsters this dichotomy with statements of approval (or coveting) by the natives themselves. Mitra, a member of the reading group, confesses "that she envied Daisy's courage" (109, 200). Razieh, the Marxist student who is later executed, says, "I don't know why people who are better off always think that those less fortunate than themselves don't want to have the good things." For Razieh these things include good music, good food, and the non-Marxist desire to read Henry James (221). Menacing Muslims such as Mr. Nyazi ("Mr. in Need") do not just covet, they become threatening. Nyazi believes that "the whole American society deserves to die" (127). The American reader is quickly assured that Nyazi and his kind do not deserve much attention. Even in their nastiness they are small and unworthy of any connection with American institutions. Responding to accusations of spying for the CIA on the part of a certain Professor Z, the author declares: "I told him [the accuser] they had no proof that the gentleman in question was a CIA agent, and in any case I doubted that the CIA would be foolish enough to employ someone like him" (119).

This massaging of the American ego becomes more harmful when essential historical facts and conditions are withheld from the reader. Not surprisingly, RLT abhors the taking of the American hostages by a group of Iranian students in 1979 (as did many members of the general Iranian public). With no mention of the public disapproval for the incident, we read the caricatured descriptions of picnics outside the occupied embassy amid shouts of "Death to America!" The reader is then told, "A tent was raised on the sidewalk filled with propaganda against America exposing its crimes around the world" (104).

Many Iranians criticized the hostage taking. Many also believe that regardless of flaws in American foreign policy, the students who occupied the embassy did wrong. However, telling the reader that the tent was filled with "propaganda" against America is not a fair representation of the material. The American reader has the right to know that items displayed in that tent reflected a broader global perception of what is known as America's use of might against those who disagree with its views and interests. The fact that hostage taking is wrong does not invalidate global perspectives on American foreign policy as merely Iranian propaganda. Surely the literature was used to promote the hostage takers' perspective, but that does not transform all the information on display into lies and fabrications.

The American reader is protected against harsh facts. The good victims in the memoir all love things American unconditionally. Manna and Nima, the newlywed students who cannot afford to rent their own apartment, buy a satellite dish and are "euphoric" about watching American classics night after night (67). Even the Ugly confess—when no one is listening—to admiring America. Miss Ruhi, one of the most "menacing" Muslim women activists in RLT, confesses that she has given her daughter a "secret name." This woman, who has spent the last two decades of her life among any number of revolutionary figures and Iran-Iraq war casualties is short of heroes and therefore names her daughter Daisy, after Daisy Miller. Why? "Because," she says, "I want my daughter to be what I never was—like Daisy. You know, courageous" (333).

The glorification of America is in the air, if not always put into words. Nassrin tells the girls in the class that her grandpa sent her Mom to an American school. " 'The American school?' echoed Sanaz, her hand lovingly playing with her hair" (53). Nassrin leaves a notebook behind for her teacher. It is not a dreadful blue like Nahvi's love letter, which we will soon talk about. It is "brilliantly colored: white with bright bubble-gum-orange stripes" and three cartoon characters. There is a note on it too, inscribed in green and purple characters. It reads, "Be Seeing you in Florida. Things Go Better with Sunshine." Who would dare to doubt that? (328)

If despite the love lavished on America we are not sure exactly where the author's sympathy lies, RLT provides a hint. Nafisi's identity is described indirectly through the voice of a trusted friend. The magician, whom we know to be frank and to have an eye for observing important details, is asked by a friend, "What is lady Professor [Nafisi] like?" He replies, "She is okay. She is very American." Then he adds a touch of European exoticism, "like an American version of Alice in Wonderland" (176). What more could we ask of the guide who has taken us into a hidden, magical world belonging to a totally different Other?

Rewarding the Good: Pleasing the Orientalist Gaze

Like its forebears, the New Orientalist narrative offers a peek into another world, one that feels excessive and imaginary. RLT demonstrates this trait. No classic felony is left out (particularly those committed against Muslim women): degradation, wife beating, rape, flogging, shooting, molestation, and more. The gaze into this "closed" world of cruel and forbidden fantasies through the sitting room in the author's house in Tehran will not be disappointed. The white, middle-class, Western reader, normally barred from entering this world, finally has a chance to slip under the veil. She or he can now see the darkest and most revealing evidence of the primitive Oriental turned dangerous by raw emotion and blind faith.

The entertaining nature of these glimpses into the forbidden world is not lost on the author. There is an awareness of the titillation it must provide for the Western reader, allowing him or her to watch these tragic acts of cruelty by the natives. The awareness is evident from the balance provided between dark events that threaten to overwhelm and the humorous, more playful incidents that keep the reader interested and engaged. Consider the last section on Austen, where two and a half pages are lavished on setting up and describing a dance scene.

The dance takes place at lunch time, in a temporary and secret society called the Dear Jane Society (named after Austen) in an empty classroom behind closed doors. The professor, along with a handpicked group of female students, is present. She is showing them the steps of a Western dance, as it would appear in a ball in *Pride and Prejudice*. She asks if anyone can dance Persian, and everyone looks at her delicate, normally withdrawing student Sanaz. Moments later, Sanaz's hesitant personality begins to transform itself in a sequence of dance movements in which the sexual overshadows every other quality. "As we laugh and joke more, she becomes bolder," explains the narrating voice. "She starts to move her head from side to side, and every part of her body asserts itself, vying for attention with other parts. Her body quivers as she takes her small steps and dances with her fingers and her hands." In case we forget the innocence and fragility at the core of the sexual transformation taking place in front of us, the commentary adds, "A special look has appeared on her face. It is daring and beckoning." Not so natural or innocent either — it is *"designed* to attract, to pull in, but at the same time it retracts and refracts with power." However, this is a power that "she loses as soon as she stops dancing." Her power of sexual allure notwithstanding, Sanaz is the same helpless fawn you have been reading about so far (265).

In case we consider this a normal dance, and thereby miss the Otherness of the performer, the author clarifies: "There are different forms of seduction, and the kind I have witnessed in Persian dancers is so unique, such a mixture of subtlety and brazenness, I cannot find a Western equivalent to compare to it." The next sentence might as well be the portrait in an odalisque painting by an eighteenth-century European artist, torturing his imagination to depict the "essence" of all Oriental women regardless of who they are. "I have seen [Iranian] women of vastly different backgrounds," the narrator adds, "take on that same expression." What is that expression? It is a "hazy, lazy, flirtatious look in their eyes." Apparently, this primal quality is as resistant to education as it is to exposure to other cultures. The author knows that because her friend Leyly, who has turned "sophisticated" through her French education, still regains this "hazy, lazy, flirtatious" manner whenever she dances. There are no words in English to describe these qualities (265).

We are not done yet. The difference is important enough to be described even though there are no words for it. This seduction is "elusive." It is "sinewy" and "tactile." It "twists, twirls, winds, and unwinds." Please do not take this as simple feminine charm; "it is calculated, it predicts its effect before another little step is taken, and then another little step." In case the description is not Othering enough, the point is reiterated: "It is flirtatious in a way Miss Daisy Miller and her likes could never dream of being" (266).

It would be helpful to know what separates the species of Miss Daisy Miller "and her likes" from that of Sanaz. But despite the extended commentary on the dance, this is not explained. In the end, the reader makes a shocking discovery, one that contradicts *RLT*'s intense dislike for the flowing robe made mandatory for women to wear in public in Iran. We are told that the robe "oddly enough adds to the allure of the movements. With each move she [Sanaz] seems to free herself from her layers of black cloth." In short, her "captivity," and struggle to "free herself" from the robe makes the robe "diaphanous" and adds to the excitement and "mystery" of her dance (266).

Contradictions

The allure and repulsion attributed to the robe in different parts of the book is symptomatic of another problem in *RLT*, that of applying contradictory approaches to a single issue. War is one such topic. Despite numerous references to the 1980 Iraqi attack on Iran, not one alludes to courage, devotion, honor, or any such qualities as motivation among the Iranians who gave their lives to resist the aggression of the monster Saddam Hussein. The Iranians going to war are described as "very young and caught up in the government propaganda that offered them a heroic and adventurous life at the front and encouraged them to join the militia, even against their parents' wishes" (208).

No doubt, a group of young, excited males rushed to the Iran-Iraq war front in response to promises of a hero's reward. Such eager, selfless soldiers arise anytime, anywhere an outside threat breaks out. Nor would anyone deny there was war propaganda. Is there ever a war without one? There is a war going on right now that the United States is waging against an "enemy" that lives thousands of miles away and was once presumed to own threatening weapons of mass destruction that we now know do not exist. Can anyone say there is no propaganda here? Do we subject it to the same intellectual scrutiny that we devote to propaganda used in wars fought by others? After all, Iranians were not the aggressors, they were the ones attacked. As much as many of us loathe war—and as much as we wished at the time that the Iran-Iraq war would end quickly—it is distressing to see the struggle so badly misrepresented. The official line of argument out of Iran at the time, not mentioned in *RLT*, was that it was not enough to recapture the city of Khorramshahr from the Iraqis. The aggressor must be made to pay for his action or he will resume his attacks the instant he has regrouped.

Saddam was a criminal who used chemical weapons against innocent people, and he must not be allowed to get away with his invasion. Does this line of argument ring a bell with regard to the current American war? Or has Saddam Hussein changed nature as a result of walking out of American grace and friendship?

The current American war is not what I wish to discuss here. Rather, I would like to draw attention to RLT's contradictory approaches to the wars it discusses. A mere four pages after we hear expressions of horror regarding the way Iranians, young and old, give their lives to the war because they have fallen for the "government propaganda," we read snippets from Henry James's biography. It is an elegant section, mostly because of the profoundly moving quotes from James about war in general. He says in relation to World War I: "The war has used up words; they have weakened, they have deteriorated like motor car tires." How right he is. Think what has happened to the word "axis" since the introduction of the expression "axis of evil."

The focus here is not on James's insights but rather on RLT's tone. The tenor, the voice, the approach to war is, suddenly, entirely different. "When still very young, James witnessed the Civil War in America," the narrating voice tells us, explaining that he was prevented from participating in this war by a mysterious backache. Then, there is reference to James's two younger brothers who "fought with *courage* and *honor*" in the war! Apparently, they were not blinded by any form of propaganda. Rather, they were honorable human beings who cared about justice and freedom (213).

Later, we read about James's own anguish over World War I raging in Europe and his efforts to lobby on behalf of the British and Belgians to get America involved. There are no condemnations of these sentiments, nor does our narrator's voice betray the slightest disagreement. If anything, we sense complete approval. A mere two pages later, the author tells us about a quotation she had written down on a pink index card to hand to her student Nassrin, which she never managed to deliver. The quote is taken from a letter that James wrote to Clare Sheridan, whose husband was killed in World War I. The central message of the quote is rebellion and the importance of allowing oneself to feel the pain of such horrible experiences. It contains a highly sentimental reference to people who are killed in war as "these admirable beings" one must "honor and celebrate" because indeed they are "our pride and our inspiration" (215).

Perhaps the author is cognizant of the contradictory reactions expressed about the two wars in such a short interval. "James's reaction to the war," we are told, has its "peculiarities." What are these peculiarities? Only one is spelled out, namely, that his "feelings and emotions were not aroused for patriotic reasons." Why are we certain that his sentiments are not tainted by patriotism? Because James's "own country, America, was not at war." This is a rather lame excuse, considering the fact that James had actually lived in England for over forty years and would eventually adopt British citizenship before his death in 1915. In other words, his approval of a war is no more saintly and superior. Only he is Henry James and not some obscure Iranian fellow whose motivations might be corrupted by "fanaticism."

I do not wish to ridicule James's sense of solidarity with the British or present him as a warmonger. However, I insist that the same standards of admiration and honor be applied to the many Iranians who were no more fond of war yet fought with their lives against Saddam's aggression. I will never forget one morning in the summer of 1987 when I was traveling on a bus in north Tehran to visit a friend. I overheard two young men who had apparently been to the war front talking. I don't know if they knew each other or just recognized another broken human being during that short bus ride and started talking. Perhaps they were not acquainted, because they expressed their fears with the kind of freedom one feels when talking to strangers. One of the voices said: "Fighting at night was the worst. I just did not want to be hit in the dark, you see. You wouldn't even know exactly which part of you was hit for a while." The other responded, "I know, but it was more frightening when those things they fired above our heads lighted up the sky. You could suddenly see everything." I did not look at them, not even when I got off. I would not have known what to do if one had had an arm or a leg missing. I can tell you for sure that neither of them had enjoyed the war, or had looked for heroism, and yet neither had run away — which is why that country is still intact.

The truth is that a considerable number of decent people, whom we might call Henry Jameses of Iran for convenience's sake, are very appreciative of these "admirable beings," who literally stopped Saddam Hussein from landing one morning at the Tehran airport. Had he done so, would the armies of the democratic and peace-loving parts of the world have come to the rescue of the Iranians? The chemicals that killed countless Iranians and Iraqi Kurds were the same "weapons of mass destruction" that we now talk about. Only it hurt masses of a different kind. It is time to write with passion and conviction about the double standards that many of us in the democratic world live with comfortably.

Crude and absolutist thoughts are not peculiar to Iranians or Muslims. One-sided positions are witnessed among the Good, too. Listen to what Mr. Ghomi, one of the leaders of the Islamic student organizations, is quoted in RLT as saying: "We are more moral, because we've experienced real evil. *We are in a war against evil!*" (195). Does this not sound familiar? Haven't people living in the United States heard this more than once over the past few years? RLT is oblivious to these similarities; it fails to apply the same standard to both sides. The perceived difference is applied even to tangible visual similarities discussed in the same section of the book, merely pages apart. Let me give you an example.

On page 302 in RLT, we read that Persian art forms have never provided us with examples of "imaginatively expressed love." Cinema is used as an example. "Even in Persian films," we are told, "when two people are supposed to be in love, you didn't really feel it in their looks and gestures." Yes, it would be great for Iranian filmmakers to enjoy the freedom they need to make their films. But even under the current circumstances, many Iranian filmmakers are expressive on the subject of love. I find Beiza'i very lyrical and enigmatic, while Mehrjcoi, Kimiya'i, and Bani Itemad are sharp and playful in this regard as well. Bani Itemad's *Nargis* and *Under the Skin of the City* are both love stories, among other things.

Four pages later, however, RLT applies a different approach to Austen with regard to expressing love: "The sense of touch that is missing from Austen's novels is replaced by a tension, an erotic texture of sounds and silences. She manages to create a feeling of longing by setting characters who want each other at odds" (306). In other words, expression of longing by means other than physical touch is a different thing to different people. For Iranian cinema, it means the absence of love. For Austen, it is artistic subtlety of expression.

In general, there are no references to any messy things in relation to the Good. There are no arguments, no tantrums, no betrayals. All the bad things happen in the camp of the fanatics. This distance from reality is noted even by the author: "I had a feeling," she says toward the end of the section on James, "that we were living in a series of fairy tales, in which all the good fairies had gone on strike, leaving us stranded in the middle of a forest not far from the wicked witch's candy house" (241).

Generic Ambiguity

RLT operates through a generic shape-shifting between fact and fiction. This play on generic ambiguity has serious implications for the information that the work brings to its readers.

As a personal memoir, the book borrows first and foremost the authority of the author's personal voice. This is a considerable sum of specialized authority. It entails her familiarity with Persian as well as Western cultures, her world travels, her expertise on Western literary tradition, her ability to speak Persian as well as English, her special family heritage in Iran, and her personal witnessing of the crucial events of the 1980s and 1990s following the revolution. This impressive list of credentials would seem to qualify the authorial voice as one to be trusted by the general reader.

However, RLT does not speak in the voice of the narrator alone. The Good, the Ugly, and the victims of the Ugly also speak a great deal. There is nothing wrong with this technique, of course. The presence of these "authentic" voices, however, removes the author's responsibility for the accuracy of the facts and the reliability of the perspectives. If a hard-liner student says that all Americans deserve to die, these words are presented as a "fact" expressed by the hard-liners themselves, not as RLT's interpretation. Was this stated in those exact words? Was it said in the context of a nasty argument, the kind in which people say terrible things to each other? How many of the other students would have agreed with this severe and bleak position? Knowing these things would not totally transform the statement, but it would qualify its reality, intensity, and capacity for being generalized. Throwing this kind of charged comment at a reader who has a limited context comes very close to misinformation.

Let me offer a less explosive example. Early on, Manna, a member of the reading group, exclaims, "About a year after the revolution, my father died of a heart attack, and then the government confiscated our house and our garden and we moved into an apartment" (14). The author is not responsible for the accuracy of this report. She is merely passing along the information that Manna has given her. However, since no clarifications are added, the general reader cannot be blamed for concluding that in postrevolutionary Iran, when someone dies their house gets confiscated. The author is free to report these words, yet is not held liable for what is implied, omitted, or possibly inaccurate within them. A tremendous amount of information can be surmised from such reporting. In this example, Manna particularly mourns the loss of the confiscated house's swimming pool and ends her statement with the words, "I never swam again." Now the reader is likely to assume that in postrevolutionary Iran there are no pools for women because they are probably not supposed to swim at all.

At the same time, because it is not strictly a work of history, RLT is not required to provide a full context for events. The author is not expected to go out of her way to check the accuracy of facts and figures. In this way, the book plays on the ambiguity of the generic territory it occupies between fact and fiction. It is and is not a factual account of what happened in the messiest, most painful, and most tumultuous moments of contemporary Iranian history.

Then enter the great Western writers: Nabokov, Austen, James, and Fitzgerald. Their voices further enforce the author's personal authority. Challenging the insights from these great minds who wrote in the "democratic" genre of the novel would be difficult. Some readers might skip the detailed literary discussions either because they are not interested in the works analyzed or are not looking for literary criticism in the book. Even for these readers — perhaps more so in the case of such readers — references to well-known literary figures lend authority to the book. Actually, these are the parts that I like, sections devoted to these writers. In these literary critical discussions, the book captures a sense of excitement generated by the transforming power of literature. Furthermore, when discussing these writers, the author knows her subject well. Most of all, the literary observations are readable because the excitement of analyzing literature removes the anger and bitterness in her tone. The condescension disappears, as does the need to treat the Ugly with "eternal contempt."

Factual Errors

Factual errors are prevalent in RLT. I start with a few more obvious ones. Mahshid is one of the girl students described in the book as being in her teens "on the eve of the revolution" (261). Elsewhere, Mahshid speaks about how things "were different" during the "Shah's time" when she should have been under ten years old, even if we take her reference to the Shah's time to mean the mid-1970s: "I felt I was in the minority and I had to guard my faith against all odds" (327). Can a person that young be conscious of "guarding" her faith?

Nassrin confesses, "We have been taught that pleasure is the great sin"

(289). Not true! Both Persian and Islamic cultures usually sanction pleasure, as long as it falls within the boundaries of the ethically acceptable. On a different note, the female students are described as "the unlikeliest of Nabokov's readers" (22). Again, not true. Iranian boys and girls read a lot of Western literature in translation. And what of the author's claim that "we lived in a culture that denied any merit to literary works" (25)? Not true of Persian culture before, during, or after the revolution. Concerning Yassi's chances of leaving Iran to study, the book says, "It was unprecedented for a girl to go abroad to study" (285). Also, not true! Many boys and girls left — and continue to leave — Iran to study abroad. The biggest obstacle they face is usually not family opposition but procuring visas, particularly to Western countries.

RLT's greatest inaccuracies are reserved for Islamic laws concerning women. Here, the work relies on misperceptions rather than the facts. Azin is going through a divorce and custody battle. We are told: "That girl [Azin's daughter] was her whole life, and you know the courts, child custody always went to the father" (286). In Iran custody battles are, as elsewhere, difficult and unpleasant, but court decisions are not automatic. They depend on many factors, including the financial and marital condition of each parent after the divorce. When the mother remarries, for example, she does endanger her right to custody.

The references to the Iran-Iraq war are often erroneous, too. We are told of "constant defeats on the battleground" and reminded that "the war was lost." Concerning Khomeini's death, the narrator observes that "after the defeat in the war and disenchantment, all he could do was die" (238, 239, 246). The records of that terrible war are not classified information. Saddam Hussein took a few cities, used his weapons against Iraqi Kurds and Iranians, fired his missiles as far as they could reach into Iran, lost control over the parts of the country that he had occupied, and finally retreated back into Iraqi territory. This was not a victory for either side to celebrate — except no more lives were lost. Talking about an Iranian defeat on the battleground is an odd way to describe this war. At best it is inaccurate, at worst angry and spiteful.

The Subtext and the Tone

RLT gradually and surely builds a subtext regarding Iran that leaves no room for anything positive. The language mocks and disrespects groups whose views differ from those upheld by the narrator. References to postrevolutionary Iranian culture have spiteful allusions to the stupidity of the masses. At the same time, things that could be taken seriously or lead to respect for the native culture are erased. The comment about Iranian cinema, which I mentioned earlier, is a typical example. The book makes a point of noting that the chief film censor in Iran is a blind — or nearly blind — man but neglects to mention that Iranian cinema is flourishing and in fact has emerged as a pioneer in twenty-first-century avant-garde film (24).

We are supposed to accept that religious legal debates in Iran occur at only the basic level of discussing forbidden sexual behavior. Therefore, thinkers and critics such as Shafi'i-Kadkani and Soroush are not mentioned because what they have to say is complicated and interesting (71). The university professor who puts literary debates to vote by show of hands believes that "the lives of intellectual men" are destroyed by "flighty females." He is presented as a typical sample from the Iranian postrevolutionary academia (69). The activist students are not any better. They set their tables outside the university almost always demanding more blood. "Never once" have their protests been "against the killings." One might ask why "the killings" took place if there were no protests by the opposition (100).

The disdain in the language the book employs colors everything, returning often to the "ruling elite's inferiority complex" (288, 27, 280). The sinister choice of words gradually becomes so familiar that it is hard to detect. Those attending Khomeini's funeral are "swarms" of mourners; the room in which the author and her students meet is "deceptively sunny"; the tall trees in front of her apartment "censor" the street, the hospital, and its visitors from view (244, 8). If you live in an apartment building in Tehran, Rome, or Istanbul, hearing the hubbub in the street is a joyful sound. It tells you that life is going on outside your window. Farrokhzad wrote about this hubbub in one of her most famous short poems. In *RLT*, however, outside the author's window there is the noise of the children, then their mothers' voices "shouting, calling out their children's names and threatening them with punishments" (8).

Lack of Compassion

In the chapter on James, there is a nice quote from Flaubert: "You should have a heart in order to feel other people's heart." The narrator is "immediately reminded of poor Mr. Ghomi, who missed all these subtleties"

(224). The spitefully remembered "poor Mr. Ghomi" is an activist Muslim student who speaks with hostility toward characters in Western novels. The message is simple: he does not have a heart. None of the Ugly are presented as having one. The memoir displays a complete lack of compassion toward the "swarms" of the Ugly who are everywhere. There are specifically gruesome examples.

A shell-shocked Muslim student, apparently returning from the war front, burns himself to death. The image of his burned body on the stretcher haunts our author (250). But there is little compassion for the young man who might have indeed killed himself out of mental illness resulting from violence he witnessed in the war. Since the author does not know much about him she speculates: "To say that he was 'active' meant that he was one of the most fanatical" (250). We are also told that the student *must* be one of the "usurpers" of a place in the university, and that he *must* have come back from the war finding the revolution in shambles and therefore decided to burn himself. Like his other comrades, the torched one has "turned himself into a revolutionary, a martyr and a war veteran, but," the book argues, "not an individual." Why is he not an individual? Because the author does not remember his name (252). Ordinarily, such oversights can be the result of a weak memory, lack of attention, or indifference. But in the case of the disturbed Muslim activist, this is evidence that he was not "an individual."

As the regime's loudspeakers urge everyone to return to their classes, our narrator tells us of her feeling "obsessed" with the incident and irritated with the Muslim activist who has turned himself into a victim, forcing everyone to take a look at his misery. For our author, however, looking does not lead to sympathy for the torched person. It leads to a question about her own irritation and resentment concerning the incident. "Had he, by burning himself, usurped our right to revenge?" is the question that emerges out of this tragic event (252).

There is another account in RLT, even more lacking in compassion. That is the group mocking of Mr. Nahvi's love letter to one of the students, Mitra. Nahvi is one of the Ugly. He is the "activist" Muslim man who has "earned eternal contempt" in the memoir by preferring the protagonist in Gorky's *Mother* to the young ladies in Austen's novels. This is the same character whom the author scorns: "I am not comparing you to Elizabeth Bennet. There is nothing of her in you to be sure—you are as different as man and mouse" (288, 290). The scorn itself—caused by the student's preference in fictional characters—is disturbing. However, these contemptuous words pale in comparison to what the memoir does to Nahvi's love story. Once again the narrator's voice and those of the girls are interwoven to bring us the story of the love letter.

A little background information helps us to make better sense of this story. The memoir has specific expectations of Nahvi and his likes. For example, they can "quote and misquote the Koran"; but reading, and quoting, a piece that Edward Said has written on *Mansfield Park*, for instance, is not expected of them. How can *they* "identify with" and "co-opt the work and theories of those considered revolutionary in the West" (289, 290). In RLT the West and Islam are homogeneous, impenetrable, and mutually exclusive entities. They must not contaminate each other.

The emotion of love seems to be equally inconceivable for a Muslim activist such as Nahvi. (In fact, the inability to fall in love is indicated as a possible side effect of Islamic activism in the case of the boy who burnt himself as well: "Did he ever fall in love?" the author asks [252].) That Nahvi has fallen in love should be a positive thing, but it is not. Furthermore, the object of his affection is Mitra, one of the author's students. Nahvi has written a love letter to Mitra, we are told, and sealed it in a "hideous blue" envelope that smells of "cheap perfume, or rosewater." "Inside the envelope, Mitra had found a one-page letter, with the same dreadful color and smell" (291). Although he has revolutionary power and influence, Nahvi does not try to use them to gain Mitra's approval. Indeed, he has not inflicted any harm beyond the color and scent of his letter. Amid ample giggling and detailed discussion of Nahvi's amusing appearance and feelings in the literature class, we wait to see what the villain does next. Sure enough, he returns with something outrageous, a beautiful quote from e. e. cummings. It is one of my favorites, too:

Somewhere I have never traveled, gladly beyond
Any experience, your eyes have their silence:
In your most frail gesture are things which enclose me,
Or which I cannot touch because they are too near

Mitra gets worried. She makes up a lie about being engaged to someone else, and Nahvi takes his poem and goes away. That is all this terrible villain does in this anecdote. He falls in love, writes a letter on blue, perfumed paper, quotes e. e. cummings, is rebuffed by the object of his affections, and goes about his life. For this behavior, he is rewarded by two pages of ridicule that denigrates everything about him from his physical appearance to the specific words he uses in his love letter. The anecdote ends with the author alluding to the fact that Nahvi learned the poem in her class. "It is enough" she says "to put you off teaching poetry" (292).

🌸 We live in the United States of America, far away from Muslim extremists such as Nahvi, Ghomi, and Nyazi. One of the undesirable impacts of the New Orientalist narrative, in this case *RLT*, is keeping us focused on these villains and enforcing the myth that all is well where we live. It is true that most of us can live, think, imagine, fall in love, use the perfume of our choice, and quote any poets we like. If we look with intent, however, the picture may turn out to be a lot more complicated.

🌸 Farrokhzad once wrote: "If you come to see me, my charming friend! Bring me a lamp and a window." This expressed her desire to see the elephant reflected, here, in the world outside her walls. It was also her way of saying we should borrow each other's windows; openings in the walls of unquestioned perceptions.

Let me gift you with my lamp and a window and ask you to greet some decent, ordinary people who, in our present-day America, live lives constrained by being Iranian or Muslim. These ordinary people do not make it into the headlines nearly as often as Mr. Nahvi and Mr. Nyazi do—all the more reason why you should take the lamp and look for them.

Please meet an Iranian graduate student separated from her elderly parents who now live in Europe. She is too anxious to talk to them; they sound too frail on the phone. If she risks leaving the United States she might not be allowed back in because she holds an Iranian passport and a student visa. If that happens, she will lose all that she has here, including the Ph.D. work she has done so far. If she stays to play it safe she might never see them again.

Please greet my Muslim colleague who made the terrible mistake of buying a one-way ticket on an airplane. She is a practicing Muslim, with beautiful, long hair pouring down her shoulders to the waist and an absolutely gorgeous Indian accent. I know a million people will agree with me when I say her smile is dazzling. Last week, she went to Chicago by car and was in a rush to return to St. Louis. She is a single mom, you see. She got herself a one-way ticket to fly back and was pulled out of line and interrogated thoroughly before she was allowed on the plane. If you are a Muslim, you should never give the impression that you do not intend to return from a journey. You will be taken seriously. "It was too careless of me to buy a one-way ticket," she said with her usual smile. "It looked suspicious."

Please meet my loving Turkish friend, whose compassion for all humanity warms up a weekly reading group I attend. She is deeply wounded by the idea of her holy book being flushed down the toilet at Guantanamo Bay, and even more hurt by the way the media brushes aside the issue of trampling her faith under foot and concentrates instead on whether the method is effective in interrogation.

Finally, I want to introduce you to a young Iranian couple who have recently moved to St. Louis. He is a physician and she a young, vibrant homemaker. They are both very literary minded, so I feel privileged to have gotten to know them. Apparently they have participated in a discussion group held on the premises of Washington University, open to the public and attended by a mix of Muslim and non-Muslim Americans. Not so long ago, an FBI agent paid a visit to their house. The agent was polite; he called before coming and stayed only about an hour asking questions about their activities, "the meetings" in particular. He also made it plain that they had been watched over the past few months. Watched? Why? They do not know. No one does. I would like to tell the couple, "Please don't take this personally." They probably prefer that I say nothing.

    I hope you honor me by keeping the lamp and the window, meeting as many people as you can, and acknowledging that indeed "genuine democracy cannot exist without the freedom to imagine without any restriction" (330).

Let me now end this extended critique of *RLT* and take you back to my jasmine and stars. In the next chapter, these include my father's Sufi saints, Princess Shirin's taming of a difficult man, and the pair of kittens who gave me the courage to reinterpret a well-known poem.

6

Tea with My Father and the Saints

I can easily compare my uncle the painter to a saint. In fact, I have a hard time imagining a saint in any other way. My father, by contrast, was not a saint by any stretch of the imagination. He was emotional, demanding, and easily offended. Our relationship, which grew closer in the latter years of his life, always remained stormy.

— Why can't you stay the whole summer?
— But, Baba, I have a family and a job in St. Louis!

We exchanged those two sentences close to a hundred times, I am sure. If he were really upset, he would add, "I won't be here when you come next time." But then he could not bear the thought of my being hurt. Big hugs, cups of tea, and stories of saints whom he loved very much and called "friends of God" were vehicles we would use to normalize our relationship. An alternative solution was asking me to read a *ghazal* of Sa'di or Hafez, after which he would declare with considerable pride, "No one reads like you." I know he meant it. When I had my radio show in Iran he listened to it every day, recording it at the same time. My cousins had a joke about going to his room and hearing me talk, whether I was there or not.

If I were to choose one adjective to describe Baba, I would say "generosity" without a moment's hesitation. He never "owned" anything, not really. Everything that he had was in his custody temporarily until a more suitable candidate could be found to receive it as a gift. The outstanding qualification for the prospective recipient was showing a flicker of interest in the object. It never was necessary to ask. That is what he liked in saints as well, their generosity and warmth toward ordinary mortals in need of divine grace. He knew a million stories about every one of the saints by heart. Each story usually included elaborate details and centered on an unbelieving individual encountering a true saint. During the encounter, the skeptic's obstinacy would be shaken by the wondrous presence of the saint. Of course the episodes would always end with complete and unconditional salvation being bestowed upon the transformed individual. Some stories he would tell again and again, each time I went back. My mother's patience would sometimes wear thin: "She knows this one! You told it the other day." Baba would continue undeterred. He did not repeat the stories because he forgot that he had told them before. His memory never faded even after the age of eighty-five. He just loved to serve as the voice for the friends of God.

I never encountered another person with such sensitivity to poetry. Baba's memory was a treasure house of the most exquisite verses that Persian poets had ever written. He recited them to himself, and us, from memory quite often. That is how I developed my first interest in poets such as Sa'di, Hafez, Rumi, and others who later became subjects of my study and work. My father was, and to this day remains, the first and best teacher of poetry I ever had. It was not just that he knew so many verses by heart. A computer can store more. It was his love for the poems, the originality of his mind, and the many ways in which he tried to understand the verses. I only needed to say, "Baba, what do you think Rumi meant by . . ." There would follow an elaborate discussion. He had invariably already thought about that very point and had come up with *his* interpretation. I did not always agree with his analysis, but I have never ceased to be amazed at the range and complexity of the ideas he had. He worked as an accountant in a bank, a job he did very well. But he had never studied literary theory in his life.

Most of our arguments were about poetry, too. I was developing my own ideas at an early age, and very fast. While a part of him was very proud of my progress, his stubborn side would not yield to this newcomer who had her own perspective on literary matters. Besides, he loved comparison, contrast, and choosing the best. I never managed to convince him not to compare works, just to enjoy every poet for who she or he was. Not surprisingly, he had his favorite among poets — who else but Sa'di, the master of *ghazal* writing. There was another reason for Baba's special admiration of Sa'di: he was a friend of God, "one who had attained the seventh station in the spiritual journey," Baba would proudly declare every time. I'll never forget the night we got into a serious argument. He defended Sa'di, and I Hafez. Only eleven or twelve, I loved both poets but argued with him just the same. This was not our first argument over poets, so I forgot about it the next day. A few days later, however, he thanked me for it. I could not believe my ears. Baba thanking me for arguing against his beloved Sa'di? The master himself had appeared to him in a dream the night of the argument and performed his morning prayer wash using water from the little pond in our yard. A friend of God preparing to pray in our house? What an unexpected blessing, even if it had only happened in a dream! My stubborn resistance had been the reason. No wonder I was quickly forgiven for this argument. Baba remembered that story, too, and told it to me last summer when I saw him in Shiraz for the last time.

Memories such as these explain my frustration with one particular stereotype reinforced through the New Orientalist narrative: that of the parrotlike Eastern mind able only to repeat but not to analyze or argue. In *Reading Lolita in Tehran* (RLT) the author tells us about an experience during her years of teaching in Iran. Correcting an exam she discovers that the entire class has transcribed her lectures word for word, complete with the occasional "you know." Astounded, she consults with colleagues who inform her that this is regular practice. The students memorize everything their teachers say and give it back to them without changing a word (RLT, 220). This is so different from my experience of Iranian boys or girls before or after the revolution. Like young people anywhere else in the world, some are more intelligent and inquisitive than others; a few are happy to take the easy way out, following the rest; yet many are prepared to argue, even fight, when they have a point to make. The revolution has not metamorphosed them into a herd of sheep. No event can do that to the youth of an entire nation.

Returning to Iran year after year, I see so many young versions of myself among friends and family. The young me loved to express her opinion. I remember being told at the age of five or six, when left with an aunt for a couple of hours, "Please don't jump on the sofa, and you can keep some of the questions you have for when I come back!" I drove people insane with questions, I am told. Baba simply sent me back to Maman after the third or fourth one, unless they were about poetry — and very often they were.

Baba loved playing chess with us, though I could never get myself interested enough to master the game. Why bother with chess when one could play such fun games trying to understand one line of Hafez? Maman jokingly called chess the game for the deaf and the dumb, because we sat for hours contemplating the chess board in silence. Now that I think about it I understand her frustration. We would go from quiet contemplations of chess moves to loud fights over poetry. She loved sensible and orderly ways of doing things. Tidying up and organizing gave her a sense of comfort. It still does. Despite her severe arthritis pain, she takes minutes to rise from her chair and still longer to reach the coffee table in the middle of the room in order to close the lid on a box of chocolate left open. How did she ever put up with my father and me, who were anything but orderly? I loved untidiness because it carried the promise of finding unexpected things, things you did not know existed. That was true of arguments with Baba, too. In the passion and untidiness of the back and forth, I found bits and pieces that would keep me thinking about a line, even a single word, for days. Besides, I never won easily. Baba did not believe that grown-ups should make things easy for kids and younger people. He would always put up his hardest fight. Always, that is, except for the time that the kittens came to the rescue of Hafez and me. I must tell you this one.

A very famous verse about Hafez (and attributed to the poet himself, with some degree of uncertainty) appears on the cover of most collections of his *ghazals*. It praises the poet for his exemplary knowledge of the Qur'an. The name Hafez means a reciter, more precisely, a memorizer of the holy book. The word Qur'an itself means recitation. Reciting parts from the holy book is a great aspect of Muslim practice associated with many happy and sad occasions in life. So good reciters are always in great demand. Many simply memorize the entire text, an undertaking that does not indicate a lack of attention to the text's meaning, contrary to widely held misperceptions. Still, memorizing the text is supposed to bring a better understanding as well as spiritual merit. For professional reciters, the memorization means they carry the tools of their trade wherever they go. The verse on the cover of the collection reads:

Love will come to your rescue if like Hafez
You can recite the Qur'an from memory, in all fourteen versions

Ever since I began to understand and love the poetry of Hafez, I have doubted that he would say such a thing. Yes, he loved and respected the Qur'an, no doubt about that. But how could a mind as complex as his say such a mediocre thing? Was life that simple? You just memorize the entire Qur'an, and love comes to your rescue? Some others might say that, but not Hafez. I always thought that there must be a different way to read this verse. I had not yet figured it out, however, and would not until the kittens incident.

It was a late afternoon in the early 1970s. I was a proud junior at Shiraz University. That afternoon I had returned home after a test and was changing in my room. My eyes caught the book of Hafez sitting on the bedside table, as it still does in many rooms in many Iranian houses to this day. The verse was teasing me: "Love will come to your rescue if like Hafez / You recite the Qur'an . . ." "There is another way to read this," I thought. "I know there is." I changed and left my room to go to the hall where we usually got together; ate breakfast, lunch, and dinner; or entertained informal guests. In the same space, we interacted with each other and with the many cats that loved our house. At any point in time we had anywhere between four and eight cats. They all had names, ate homemade food courtesy of Maman, and roamed the entire neighborhood. As to our house, the word "old" would not do it justice. The building was ancient, two stories, with relatively small rooms and high ceilings and plenty of nooks and crannies to explore. I loved the garden, overcrowded with orange and pomegranate trees. A stream had once run through the side of the yard, reminiscent of the days when the neighborhood consisted of gardens. Alas, the gardens had turned into houses, and the stream did not flow anymore. On the other side of the yard, by the hothouse, stood another relic from old days: a well. No one had used water from a well in Shiraz for some time now, but the well was there all the same, dry and covered up. Or at least that was what we thought.

Day or night, our house could be filled with any number of visiting friends and relatives. There were hardly any specified times for visits. That afternoon, I walked to join whoever might be in the hall besides Maman. My mother would sit on a chair talking to the guests. On the way I passed Baba's room, where he would usually be sitting on his bed if not in the hall. He would be sharpening a new reed pen for calligraphy, doing crossword puzzles, listening to the radio, or reading a book. Hearing my footsteps, he would declare, "You're back," with a satisfied look on his face, then ask a word for his puzzle, or better still, burst into a story about a saint. Maman would interfere at some point, particularly if I had not had lunch. "Let her eat something first," she would say. "Would you like a cup of tea, Fati Joon?" That is their pet name for me, Fati Joon. I loved their attention. All during my high school years I studied in the hall or the kitchen because I loved the feeling of having my mother close by. It did not mean that I was not independent or had no conflicts with my parents. We had plenty of disagreements, particularly when I went through with my divorce against their will. But love was the current running through the background.

The door to Baba's room was open as usual. He was not there, nor was he in the hall. "He has been trying to get the kittens out. I was helping him until a few minutes ago myself," explained Maman. Which kittens? Out of where? Something must have happened. Playing with the kittens in the yard was not something Baba would do on a hot afternoon early in the fall. Yes, something had indeed happened. Two of the youngest kittens, of which we always had a healthy pack, were missing. Although Baba did not generally play with the kittens, he always monitored their growth and well-being. Noticing their absence, he had spent the whole morning searching for them. He finally found them alive, trapped at the bottom of the dried-up well next to the hothouse. They must have been playing and had literally fallen through the cracks. I rushed to the yard. "Salaam, Baba! Can I help?" I asked. He mumbled an uncharacteristically quiet salaam and asked for a glass of water. My services were obviously not in demand. He was too busy trying to make changes to the little basket he kept sending down the well. That was the easy part. The hard part was tempting the kittens to get in and stay put as they were being pulled out. "Thank goodness they are off their mother's milk," he declared with a fairly serious face, "or they would be dead by now." I asked him to call me if he needed help and returned to the hall, where I was greeted with a steaming cup of tea and the little silver bowl filled with sugar cubes.

By early evening, Baba did not need my help at all. The saga of the kittens had traveled beyond the house and a few eager cousins had joined the rescue mission. We even had youngsters volunteering to go down the well and carry the victims to the top. But Baba objected vehemently to this plan. Wells, particularly the old ones, were not to be trusted. They had their mysteries. He remembered well diggers from his early days who had fallen unconscious at the bottom of the well they were digging and even lost their lives. He was too busy to relate a story, but none of the brave cousins were given permission to descend into the well. Alas, the kittens were determined not to leave their prison, although they did not seem to enjoy it much, judging by their incessant meowing. Fortunately, they had not gone on hunger strike and ate the food that was sent down in large amounts, perhaps too frequently. Without realizing why, I stayed awake for a while that night obsessing about the verse on the cover of the book next to my bed: "Love will come to your rescue . . ." "There is surely another way to read this," I thought as I drifted into sleep.

When I left for the university the next morning, Baba was a one-man operation again. I don't know how Maman had persuaded him to give it a break for the night. He had started all over again right after breakfast. By the time I returned home that afternoon, Baba had found a basket so large that the kittens had to climb in if they wanted to reach the food at its center. Furthermore, he had cut the edges low for the kittens to be able to climb over and yet high enough to protect them from falling out as they were lifted to safety. Sure enough, sometime before dark, Baba had pulled both kittens out of the well. He had changed his clothes and now sat on a chair in the hall with a big cup of tea in front of him and a bigger smile on his face. His eyes were teary. I was used to that. Maman would never cry unless she was truly hurt or angry about something. I can count the number of times I have seen her crying. Not with Baba. He was big on tears. It did not matter whether the story involved the generosity of a saint or a pair of kittens rescued from the well. Tears would roll down his cheeks and make his voice tremble with emotion. I gave him a big hug, which he happily accepted, before I rushed to my room to prepare for a test the next day. Calls were coming in from cousins inquiring about the kittens. Baba did not forget to include an embellished description of the rescue basket as he accepted compliments for saving the little things.

Back in my room, the verse on the cover of the book caught my eye again as I took out my notes to study: "Love will come to your rescue if like Hafez . . ." Of course! How could I not see it? How on earth could I not see it before? Why did it take me so long? Was it Baba's tears, the glittering eyes of the rescued kittens, the hitting of my head against the wall for that long? I did not know. It didn't matter either. Suddenly I knew. I knew how to read that verse beyond a shadow of doubt. It was not the Qur'an Hafez was talking about at all. It was love. He had put the Qur'an in there only in order to elevate love above the holiest of holies, the word of God himself. He wanted the verse to be read with stress on the word love, which would insert an "even if" into the rest of the line. With the change in intonation, the verse would mean:

Love [is that which in the end] will come to your rescue [even] if like Hafez
You can recite the Qur'an from memory, in all fourteen versions

Some people might disagree, but Baba would understand. I ran to the hall. He was still there, happy and teary-eyed, enjoying his cup of tea. "Baba,

Baba, I solved the problem!" I said, my voice shaking with excitement. "They haven't fallen back in there again, have they?" was his first reaction. "No, Baba, I am not talking about the kittens. It is the verse of Hafez I was telling you I don't like." He remembered immediately; he always did. Encouraged with his recollection I continued, "You shouldn't read it as if it means love will come to your rescue only if you know the Qur'an by heart." He remembered that too and wanted to know what my solution was. I took a second then proudly presented the solution, reciting the verse softly and with the stress on the right words. It took him only seconds. He never needed longer. Then there was the familiar flash in his eyes, the one that combined laughter and tears, indicating that he had recognized the magic of a verse. "You have that one right," he conceded quietly and immediately. No arguments at all. He repeated the verse — with the new emphasis — to himself a few times and reinstated his approval, "You have it right." I sat there for a minute longer, enjoying the echo of the new reading in my thoughts with the relief of someone who has found a precious object that has been missing for some time. How did I think for one instant that Hafez would say it any other way? Then Baba's words broke my train of thought: "They are both okay, both." No, he couldn't do that. He could not withdraw his approval. Besides, who else would understand it if he didn't? "No, Baba! He couldn't have meant it both ways. His mention of the Qur'an is . . ." He interrupted, "O, I meant the kittens. I was afraid only one would get in the basket but they both did." I walked back to my room quietly, leaving him alone with his cup of tea. He did not need a reminder on the way love comes to the rescue. Not that night.

We did not always talk about mystical poets such as Hafez and Saʿdi. Both of us loved a wide range of poetry. Versified stories were among Baba's favorite kinds of literature. Among the protagonists of such stories, he loved Shirin, the heroine of the romantic epic in rhyming couplets, *Shirin and Khusrau*. She appealed to the unsaintly side of his character. The master poet/storyteller Nizami of Ganjeh (twelfth century CE), who wrote the love story, had given Shirin's personality all the charm of his own beloved wife, Afaq, whom he used as a model. The story has many complex and fascinating characters. But to my father, as to Nizami himself, it was all about Shirin.

Shirin is a neighboring princess who falls in love with the Persian king Khusrau after seeing a portrait of him. She gets on her horse and rides for fourteen days to reach Iran in pursuit of her love. They fall in love after seeing each other. However, they have to overcome many hurdles before they are able to unite. Many of these problems are caused by Khusrau's stubborn, princely nature. He is courageous, good-looking, spoiled, and intoxicated with power. She is beautiful, mature, equally courageous, and proud. She loves Khusrau but knows that he is not yet ready to be her companion, nor an effective king for his own country. He has much to learn.

Farhad is the third major character introduced to the story. He is an artist, a stonemason. Initially, he is brought in to design a passageway to bring milk from where the cattle are kept to Shirin's palace for her breakfast. But he, too, falls in love. Who can resist Shirin's impeccable beauty and charisma? Shirin's reaction to Farhad is interesting. She never doubts her own love for Khusrau but admires Farhad's artistic sophistication and re-finement. He is quiet, thoughtful, selfless, and imaginative—the opposite of Khusrau. She likes that. Shirin's own personality possesses the strengths mirrored in the character of both lovers and is never overwhelmed by the love and attention from either. One day, visiting Farhad, who is working on the palace, she is so impressed with the quality of his work that she takes her ruby earring off and gives it to him. Hearing about it, the king is jealous. He sends someone to announce the false news of Shirin's death to Farhad, who consequently ends his own life. Khusrau and Shirin marry, and they live together for many years. During these years Shirin has a great impact on Khusrau's personality. The love story is a tragedy and ends in the couple's death; nevertheless, their time together is happy, full of lively and hu-morous exchanges. I remember my father reciting passages from the story by heart. These were mostly passages that had to do with Farhad's longing for Shirin, or Shirin's exquisite beauty and wisdom. I do not think he was very fond of Khusrau. When I was young, I once said, "Baba, did Shirin really exist?" He looked at me with a straight face and said: "Only for about eight hundred years." Then he laughed and added: "A lot of people know her." He often liked to tease me. It took a while before I realized he had been serious this time.

Beauty and resilience were core qualities I continued to associate with Shirin's personality. Indeed, it might have been to join all those people who had known and admired her throughout her eight hundred years of life that I contributed an essay about her to the volume *Women in Iran: From the Rise of Islam to 1800.*

As I grew into an adult woman, however, I redefined Shirin for myself. My father had related to her as a man would to a virtuous and charming woman. I reinvented her step by step until she became an exciting model of womanhood, one that was uniquely mine. She could stop during a fourteen-day, lonesome journey on horseback, tie her horse to a tree, undress, and bathe in the spring without fear. Yet, in the water, her bare skin was as delicate as a water lily. Besides personal admiration for courage, I had another compelling reason to cherish the warrior aspect of Shirin's character.

Living in the West, faced with demeaning stereotypical representations of myself as an Iranian Muslim woman, I needed women who stood out in memory, who made me feel empowered. There she was, beautiful, caring, decisive, and wise; a counterimage for the media-concocted New Orientalist narration of me that said I would be happier isolated and suppressed. I remember reading the reaction of Manna, one of the students in RLT's reading group, to Vincente Minnelli's *Designing Women*: "It occurred to her that she had never imaginatively experienced love in a Persian context" (RLT, 302). Manna's feelings are further described by the author, "She had never heard a love song, read a novel or seen a film that made her think that this could be her experience."

I could read such comments and think: not me! I never felt alien to this worldly love. True, I had started with admiring the archetypal figure of Shirin. But it had led me to parallels among my own contemporaries: not just Farrokhzad and Behbahani, but figures in major works of fiction, such as Yousof and Zari in Danishvar's best-selling novel *Savushun*. Danishvar herself had made history by selling close to half a million copies of her novel, a record in the 1970s. She has continued her success as a major writer after the 1979 revolution.

These women, as well as men, helped me understand love as a most natural component of life. Yousof and Zari's relationship in *Savushun*, for example, had a powerful physical component, and took place in the twentieth century in Shiraz. It could be my own story. Then my interest in cinema added a new dimension, a different opportunity to experience rich new layers of artistic expression exploring the emotion of love. Beiza'i's wonderful, classic love story of Persian cinema *Ragbar* ("The Downpour") is still a favorite that I share with students in advanced Persian.

I enjoyed many non-Persian writers, too, but was fortunate not to have to wait for Vincente Minnelli to come along and show me an example of imaginatively expressed love. I already had a deep familiarity with artistic ways of speaking about this significant emotion, as well as its personal and interpersonal dimensions. In RLT, Manna and Nima seem to be happily married, but they feel they do not know anything about love. They are together because neither has anyone else to talk to and because "misery loves company—and can be as strong a force as love" (RLT, 303). I had gone through an arranged marriage, and a divorce, yet I had not felt unable to understand or experience love. I could see Shirin, bathing in the cool spring water during her journey to Iran, and as flowers can grow in water, she grew for me. No, her significance did not just come from the fact that she lived eight hundred years and so many people knew her. She was the resilient flower that came back every season, blooming in her distinct womanhood with new, fascinating colors.

When I look at the essay I wrote about her, I see this personal dimension; affirming my womanhood through writing about hers. I devoted the piece to two human characteristics that are often viewed as contradictory in women: the capacity to love and the ability to educate. To make sure the point stood out, I called the essay: "Taming of the Unruly King: Nizami's Shirin as Lover and Educator." Describing Shirin's character, I wrote:

> An intriguing characteristic of Shirin's wise and stable personality is its apparent lack of conflict with sexual desire and attraction. All major belief systems demonstrate suspicion toward female sexuality and at best consider it a source of distraction and temptation. This sexual potency is equally exaggerated in literary traditions. Women's sexually magnetic power can make men lose their ability to judge and leave them susceptible to committing irreversible errors. It is not surprising that such dangerous beings have not often been portrayed as educators or sources of wisdom and knowledge—or have achieved that status only after aging and losing their initial physical attraction. Shirin, however, is beautiful and desirable. Her ruby lips, dark hair, and fragrant body are frequently and graphically described. They are not meant to have any mystical or spiritual connotations and at times are clearly and unquestionably erotic.

Then I went on to discuss Nizami's attention to Shirin's sexuality while describing the lovers' wedding night. Shirin has asked Khusrau not to drink that evening so they can have a sober and full appreciation of their first intimate contact. Knowing Khusrau's obstinacy, Shirin puts an old woman in her place to test Khusrau's sobriety. Predictably, Khusrau has broken his promise. But he discovers the ruse because Shirin's charm is unmistakable! After her beauty is described elaborately once more, Shirin finally enters the nuptial chamber. I ended with the following: "The description of the lovers' first intimacy is probably one of the most lavishly detailed erotic descriptions of lovemaking in classical Persian literature."

Her magnificent, female, carnal charm does not detract a bit from Shirin's strength of personality. On one occasion before they are married, Khusrau — who has been ticked off by Shirin's pride — has been disloyal. Obviously, Shirin has taken offense. The king regrets his action and returns apologetic to the door of her palace asking to see her. He speaks from behind the closed door:

> Open the door, after all, this is the king!
> He has come on foot to apologize to you.
> You know that in my farthest thoughts
> I would not dream of doing you any wrong.
> You have to sit with me for a while!
> I cannot go before seeing your face.
> But if you so wish I leave this place in haste,
> Allow me [at least] to take one look at you head to foot!

Shirin appears on the terrace and speaks to the king kindly. Despite her kind words, however, she does not open the door for him to come in. Khusrau's promiscuity is unacceptable. If he wants her love, he needs to change. Nizami takes care to demonstrate to us, in the extended narrative plot, that he actually does change. I remember Baba's smile one more time: "She lived eight hundred years. A lot of people knew her." He is so right.

The question, "To whom does Shirin belong?" is an interesting one. It is also a question we do not pose often because its answer seems clear: she belongs to those who lived eight hundred years ago. Living in a world influenced by challenges of the globalized free market has its great advantages, but it also holds disadvantages. One disadvantage is the feeling that one has to be always guessing what might catch the attention of future buyers (it does not matter what is for sale: goods, services, or ideas). This desperate need to get ahead of the future sometimes leads to simplistic projections of time in which the past and the future are treated as opposites.

According to this worldview, one has to be backward looking to enjoy the artistic and cultural intricacies of premodern times. Similarly, in order to move forward, one is expected to focus on current topics only. Those of us who often teach things medieval are always on the lookout for ways to show our students that the past can be pointing right to the future. Alas, this is not an easy point to sell to every bright undergraduate. We do not easily give up, though. The beauty and attraction of Shirin, along with the elegance of Nizami's love story, provide powerful tools for teaching the complicated fact that the past helps us make sense of the future.

Many of us who come from the Middle East and specialize in medieval literature work doubly hard to ensure that we are not backward-looking technophobes. It is certainly hard to keep up with bright undergraduates of the twenty-first century who seem to catch up with new technology before it is invented. I make a special effort to display my up-to-date computer skills. I am even the proud personal designer of my own Web sites. Not that they cannot be improved. But I have constructed them myself. Compliments on the Web sites, particularly from the students, are most enthusiastically accepted. There is one fruit of technology, however, that I have not quite come to terms with, namely television. It is less and less of a threat at this point in my life. In fact, I can easily avoid it now. But I always shudder at the thought of television coming to my hometown in Shiraz a few years earlier than it actually did. Had this great invention, which thrilled many people, entered our house earlier, it would have stolen some precious things from my childhood. It would certainly have taken away a good many rounds of evening tea with my father and the saints who visited regularly. I would like to share with you some of their treasures before this book ends.

At no point in my life, either in childhood or later, has mysticism ever been a mere fog on a distant mountain. It has not been a set of abstract and intangible exercises in philosophizing about the afterlife. The saints who visited us at tea time were absolutely real people with real concerns about everyday things. They cared about the impact of their actions and words. They spoke with the utmost frankness, and there was an overpowering beauty in the simplicity and passion of their words. In a way, they were paradoxical beings. They were like a towering mountain peak with a sincere desire to stay close. Perhaps the best metaphor to describe them is that of a small stream that sings a carefree song as it runs by your house. It is so nonthreatening that you can sit by it, look at your reflection in the water, and even wash your hands in it. It is yours, your personal stream. Yet you know that it has originated in the sea and is on its way back to where it has come from. When passing by your house, however, it is yours. You can say it is a personal moment you have torn out of eternity to keep in your pocket for yourself. However, I must stop short of describing Sufi saints, their wisdom and their manner. They speak eloquently for themselves, as you would know best only after you conversed with them yourself. How would I ever have met any of them if television, or any other distraction, had arrived at our house first and closed the door on the saints who visited us for tea?

This is how they came. After dinner was over, probably around 7:30 or 8:00 in the evening, we would sometimes drink tea as we listened to music on the radio. My parents were fond of music and had their favorites. Alternatively, friends and relatives would stop by, in which case we would drink tea and talk with them. On the nights that neither of these things happened, we would drink tea and my father would take his copy of the *Memorials of the Saints*, by Attar, the medieval poet and biographer of Nishabur, off the shelf. He would dust the cover and open the book in front of him. As early as I can remember, I would plant myself squarely before him and wait for one of my favorite saints to show up.

Bayazid, the Sufi master of Khurasan, who deliberately ate in public one day during Ramadan to free himself of the saintly image he had developed within the community, was one. I loved Bayazid for his frankness, among other things. He once said to a young disciple who wanted a small cutting from his sheepskin coat to keep as a blessing: "It wouldn't do you any good if you pulled my own skin over yourself. If you like what you see in me, do what I do." But he was not always this harsh. Most of the time, he was a poet. "I was out in the fields," he once said. "Love had poured down and the earth was moist. Just as feet sink into mud, my feet sank into love." I was too young to understand any of the mystical or literary connotations of these words, but these were just like the words that my singing dervish used in his songs as he passed through the alleyway late at night. I knew that Bayazid was speaking of something that was very near and definitely related to my life. Later, when I learned to write, I wrote the sentence about sinking into love and stuck it on the wall of my room. There were other things, things I carried in my memory for years before I could make enough sense of them or have a place to put them. "I have never seen a light as bright as silence," Bayazid once said. Another time he declared publicly, "Glory be to me, how great is my state!" and apparently was thrown out of town for a while because this was the standard parase used to glorify God! The inhabitants of his hometown of Bistam must have liked him a lot, because they took him back every time he broke a rule or pushed the limits.

Another Sufi saint I liked a lot was Junayd of Baghdad. Unlike some other Sufis who owned little, Junayd was relatively well off. One day, a poor man who had stolen some of his clothes was trying to sell a shirt in a second-hand store at the local market. The shopkeeper took one look at his scruffy appearance and said, "How do I know you haven't stolen this nice shirt?" "How can I prove it is mine?" asked the thief. "I need at least one witness," demanded the potential buyer. Junayd who was passing by testified to the man's ownership of the shirt. And, of course, that was the last time the man stole anything. Baba read every anecdote as if it were a well-documented historical occurrence. When saints displayed generosity, he would take his glasses off, wipe a tear, and continue to read. It took a long time before I realized that the significance of these anecdotes lay not in their factuality but in the values they carried in them, and in the way they had been treasured for generation after generation, much like Shirin's feminine charm and courage.

I sometimes argued with the saints, too. I once said to Baba, "But would-n't Junayd be lying to the shopkeeper who was now buying a stolen thing?" He took a somewhat serious look at my face over the top of his glasses and said, "If the owner said the shirt belonged to the man, it wouldn't be a stolen thing anymore, would it?" and resumed his reading. It was so simple now that he had said it. "Of course," I said to myself, "why didn't I think of that?" I had not quite finished with that thought yet when Baba paused for a second time, noting, "But you realize that Junayd is not really talking to the shop-keeper. It is the thief he is teaching a lesson to." No, I hadn't realized that. What a clever guy this Junayd was. I eagerly waited to hear the other things he had said and done. But Baba did not seem to be in a hurry. He had barely read two more sentences when he paused for the third time and said, "The person he is really teaching a lesson to is himself, though." One thing was clear, I could not blame myself for not having guessed this one. Now I was lost. How could he be teaching himself a lesson by testifying that his own stolen shirt belonged to the thief? Couldn't he simply give away a shirt that was not yet stolen to practice generosity? I was not one to give up easily. "Is it easier to give a pencil to a friend or see your pencil in someone's hand and say nothing?" Ok. I understood the general idea and lived with it for quite a while. Years later, another Sufi saint, this time my very own Rumi, shed a different interpretive light on that anecdote. In fact he was not talking about Junayd's stolen shirt but the concept of giving in general.

Rumi loves metaphors and is a magician when it comes to breathing life into them. He knows it, too. So he has developed a great metaphor to describe his art of making metaphors. "Wondrous birds grow from the palm of my hands," he once said in a poem referring to the magical quality of the images in his poetry. Here is the metaphor he uses to explain what giving and generosity do for the person who gives: The Truth is like the sun. It shines on everything indiscriminately. The trouble is you wear too many layers and do not let the sun touch your skin. Ideally, you should go completely naked because this sun does not burn. However, if that is too hard to do, at least peel off a few layers and taste the warmth of the divine sun. That was what Junayd was doing, peeling off layers to taste the sun. No wonder Baba had said his main aim was to do something for himself. Just when I thought I had finally got to the bottom of the shirt business, I stumbled on another verse of Rumi that was subverting the whole idea shamelessly and unapologetically. Owning or not owning things didn't matter at all, he was now saying. What made all the difference was the place we chose in which to store the things we owned. I almost said, you guys seemed a lot easier to figure out when you dropped by to have tea with Baba and me. What do I do with the blessed shirt now? Do I give it away, or do I not give it away?

But Sufi saints could not be hurried into doing things. In fact, they took their time with the smallest of matters. Perhaps that was the greatest difference between these figures and the characters on TV. The saints would not lower their standard to entertain, which made them most entertaining. And they were not in the habit of apologizing either. The reason was simple. Sometimes, there were important, and relevant, truths that I needed to hear. In that case, what could Rumi do except tell me? However, he did something else to make it easier to digest, the thing he does so well. He would include one of his rare metaphors every time, sending me away to do my own thinking until I found the answer. That is what is so great about metaphors as conceptual containers. There is always room left in them for you to personally fill. Here is Rumi's metaphor stressing the significance of the place in which you keep your belongings. When it is underneath the boat, he said, water serves as the means of keeping the vessel moving. The same water will sink the boat if it gets inside. In other words, ownership is about how much you love your things (literally, how much you let them get inside your heart). Complete destitution will not get you anywhere if you are totally attached to the few things you own, whereas you can own things without becoming a slave to them. In this scheme of things, the true layers you need to peel off are pride, hatred, anger, the need to seek others' approval, and the like. There is no glory in having nothing. The trick is to use things like water under your boat; whether you need to keep your shirt or to give it away is something only you can figure out.

I must wrap up this chapter and, with it, the search for jasmine and stars. Let me tell you why I loved to have tea with Rumi so much. He never tried to make things easier than they needed to be, but he never applied guilt, sadness, or punishment to impel people to be good. In fact, one of his master metaphors relates to the emotion of sadness: "That thief," he said, "has been hanged on my threshold a long time ago." And a thief it is. No one will deny sadness has stolen his or her energy at one time or another. Rumi's favorite tool for discovering the meaning of life is hope. He once observed, "hope is the beginning of the road to safety. If you can't step on the road, at least stay close."

Like all other saints who dropped by for tea, Rumi's favorite challenge, what you would give your shirt away — or peel layers off — to learn, was discovering purity of intention. The word Sufis use for this is *ikhlas* or *rasti*, being truly who you are. Rumi did not bother to try and explain the complicated concept. You have to figure it out for yourself anyway. But he provided another one of his metaphors for those who felt too weak to attempt the heroic act of being simply themselves. Don't waste so much time wondering what you have done wrong in the past, he said. Just be true to yourself and that will take care of it all. The wrongs you have done are like the little serpents that the Pharoah's magicians once produced, while being true and pure in intentions is more like the rod of Moses. It will swallow them all. In other words, life is too short for crying over what you did wrong. Just get on with what is left. And get on with it truthfully.

Finally, I want to show you one more star that brightens the road wherever I happen to be walking. I want you to meet him because he has always been an embodiment of the concept of *ikhlas* to me. When I lie down in my bed in St. Louis, Missouri, and imagine the starry skies of the midsummer nights in Shiraz, he occupies a corner of his own. Gentle and modest but brightly present, as he was in life. I call him *Amu Vazin* —

literally Uncle Vazin. He is not really my uncle. He was married to my aunt, my mother's younger sister. Like my uncle the painter, he was an army officer. In fact, the two met in the military academy in Shiraz. That is how Amu Vazin came to know our family and eventually marry my aunt. He was a person of great integrity and generosity. I can see now that, in his simple and unpretentious way, he was a great example of someone who listened to what the masters who dropped by for tea had to say. He had listened so well that he began to live that "purity of intention" in his everyday life. He was not a poet, a storyteller, a painter, or a philosopher. He was a simple person who understood the complexity of *ikhlas*, not as a fog on a mountain but as a practical guide, a tool to be used to resolve difficult problems in life.

Amu Vazin's *ikhlas* helped him overcome many difficult and undesirable conditions. One was a military conflict that could have led to the loss of many lives in the early 1960s. There had been major unrest in the streets as a result of an uprising among the nomadic *Qashqa'i* people who resided outside Shiraz. During my childhood, the rebellion erupted into street fights from time to time. The army usually moved in and, following some clashes and a few arrests, put an end to demonstrations. This time, Amu Vazin had been given the command of a battalion to chase away the rebel leaders who were now camping on the outskirts of Shiraz. Perfectly in line with his temperament, he had suggested to the rebel leaders to negotiate an end to hostilities. Nomadic people were not particularly fond of the ways of the city-dwellers and wished to preserve their own lifestyle. Besides, their commanders did not trust army officers, who were viewed not only as agents of the government but also as persons seriously lacking courage and honor. The leader of the uprising said, "How do I know that if I come to your side to negotiate, I will not fall into a trap? I don't trust you." Amu Vazin said, "Would you set a trap for me, if I come to your side unarmed?" "Of course not," replied the commander, "we are men of honor." Amu Vazin responded, "I trust you," and walked right into the rebels' camp unarmed and unaccompanied by any soldiers. The peace they negotiated that day lasted for some time. When the revolution of 1979 broke out, a lot of army officers who had had dealings earlier with the nomadic people residing on the outskirts of Shiraz were afraid of retaliation. Not Amu Vazin. He was as serene as a pond untroubled by the breeze. No one would come after him.

But this is not the reason why I remember him now in my concluding pages. I remember him for his jests and jokes. At the end of the day, when he took off his army uniform and slipped into civilian clothes, he had one mission only: to make us all laugh. You could see him walk down the street in his uniform and never guess that the night before he had done cartwheels in the middle of a semiformal party! He could not stand the put-on air of importance and seriousness. Yet he took us kids and our interests most seriously. I wrote poems from early on. He would always inquire after my latest poem, asking me to read it to him. Unlike my father and my uncle the painter, Amu Vazin had not had an extensive literary education. Yet he understood and appreciated the subtleties of poetry well. "For me, Amujan (as he would address me), read the poem a trifle slower." Then he would listen as attentively as he had to the concerns of the nomadic commander on the day of negotiations.

The last few times I visited Iran, Amu Vazin was affected by Alzheimer's disease, and his health was deteriorating rapidly. The man whose face used to light up when I opened the door of the house to him no longer recognized me. I knew it was the illness, but still I blamed myself for having been away too long. Not recognizing me was bad enough, but the worst was that he had lost his laughter. He did not joke or even smile anymore. Four years ago, when he passed away, I wrote the poem "My uncle who lost his shoes." He would not have been able to read it, even if he were alive, but capturing his laughter gave me great comfort. I would like you to meet him properly before you put away this book.

MY UNCLE WHO LOST HIS SHOES

They first knew something was wrong
When one day — after a visit to the local shrine
He came home wearing someone else's shoes.
People entered shrines barefoot for total respect
And put their shoes back on as they left.

I loved that shrine myself — when I was seven or eight.
My mother's face looked kinder
In the light that bounced off the million mirror pieces decorating the
    walls.
And the cool shiny marble floor felt wonderful
Under my bare feet.

In so much light,
He had failed to recognize his own shoes.

　　*　*　*

A few months later,
He disappeared for three days
Unable to find his way back home — perhaps from the same shrine.
When he finally had returned,
His hair and clothes had been covered with dust
And his shoes had been torn.
He had looked calm and no one had asked where he had been.

　　*　*　*

The rest was the old story:
Losing it bit by bit
Until his eyes filled with a dazed suspicion
That he ought to know the many faces he could not recognize
Or, that he should perhaps not have said
What he just did.
Some things survived the reign of confusion
His gracious manner of greeting the guests, for instance
His neatly combed hair
Or, his clean carefully pressed gray suits.

Other things slipped off the uneven edges of struggle and vanished
Into the sea of pain
That inched its way into his lonely days.
Yet others simply fell by the way side
Not the least his laughter.

　　*　*　*

That is what I miss most, his laughter, his jests
The funny faces he used to make
His flat, sometimes improper, jokes
My aunt's gentle rebuke: *charand nagu jun Vazin!*
"Don't talk nonsense Dear!"
His murmuring reply of discontent untainted by bitterness

And his immediate attempt
To find another way to make us laugh.

It feels dark this afternoon
I wonder if I would recognize my shoes
In this light

Index

Fatemeh Keshavarz, *Jasmine and Stars: Reading More than "Lolita" in Tehran* (2007).

Scott Kugle, *Sufis and Saints' Bodies: Mysticism, Corporeality, and Sacred Power in Islam* (2007).

Roxani Eleni Margariti, *Aden and the Indian Ocean Trade: 150 Years in the Life of a Medieval Arabian Port* (2007).

Sufia M. Uddin, *Constructing Bangladesh: Religion, Ethnicity, and Language in an Islamic Nation* (2006).

Omid Safi, *The Politics of Knowledge in Premodern Islam: Negotiating Ideology and Religious Inquiry* (2006).

Ebrahim Moosa, *Ghazālī and the Poetics of Imagination* (2005).

miriam cooke and Bruce B. Lawrence, eds., *Muslim Networks from Hajj to Hip Hop* (2005).

Carl W. Ernst, *Following Muhammad: Rethinking Islam in the Contemporary World* (2003).